*Modern Manners*

# MODERN MANNERS

*An Etiquette Book for*
*Rude People*

## P. J. O'ROURKE

A MORGAN ENTREKIN BOOK
THE ATLANTIC MONTHLY PRESS
NEW YORK

Chapter 8 originally appeared, in somewhat modified form, in the
November 12, 1981, issue of *Rolling Stone* under the title "Modern
Manners: Beyond Cocktail Courtesy." Chapter 21 also appeared in
*Rolling Stone*, in the September 30, 1982, issue, as "How to Get a Good
Job." Chapter 26 appeared in the Spring 1983 issue of *Playboy Fashion*
under the title "How to Dress Rich." The author thanks both publica-
tions for their permission to reprint this material.

The author would like to thank Morgan Entrekin, Terry McDonell,
Susan Moldow, Robert Neubecker, Alan Rose, and Amy Lumet for their
ideas and encouragement.

Illustration of dog's head on title page by Earl Schuler.

*Published simultaneously in Canada*
*First Atlantic Monthly Press edition, June 1989*
*Printed in the United States of America*

Library of Congress Cataloging-in-Publication Data

O'Rourke, P. J.
Modern manners / by P. J. O'Rourke.—1st Atlantic Monthly Press ed.
"A Morgan Entrekin book."
ISBN 0-87113-313-X
1. Etiquette—Humor. I. Title.
PN6231.E8076  1988     818'.5402—dc19     88-31834

DESIGN BY LAURA HOUGH

THE ATLANTIC MONTHLY PRESS
19 UNION SQUARE WEST
NEW YORK, NY 10003

THIRD PRINTING

To Lally and Katherine and Pamela Weymouth,
who have the old-fashioned kind.

# *Contents*

ix

# Contents

# Contents

xi

# Contents

*"A gentleman is one who never inflicts pain."*
                                        —Cardinal Newman

*"Unintentionally."*

                                        —Oscar Wilde

# Manners—Why Have the Things at All?

The modern world is a horrid place. It lacks anything enduring and true. It is devoid of every tenable value.

All existence is in disarray. Religious beliefs are no longer believed. Love is much discussed but little practiced. Morals are in confusion when they are in evidence at all. And intellect is no consolation: modern intelligence has become well-nigh unintelligible.

Given that life is such a mess, why should anyone care which fork is for the oysters? And yet this may be the only thing we *can* care about. Just as cleanliness becomes more important at moments when godliness is not possible, so manners come to the fore when more august forms of authority collapse. When substance is execrable, we must make form do the work of content. The world is going to hell. All we can do is look good on the trip.

# Section I

## RULES TO LIVE BY IN A
## WORLD WITH NO RULES

*Oh, let us love our occupations,*
*Bless the squire and his relations,*
*Live upon our daily rations,*
*And always know our proper stations.*
—Charles Dickens

# 1

# What Are Manners?

*In my mind, there is nothing so illiberal and so
ill bred, as audible laughter.*

—Lord Chesterfield

$\mathcal{M}$anners are a way to express altruism in daily life. Either that or manners are a way to screw people over without their knowing it. Anyway, manners are what your mother always wanted you to have. Whether your mother is a noble idealist or a scheming bitch is something that must be decided by you.

3

# HOW CAN GOOD MANNERS BE IDENTIFIED?

Good manners are a combination of intelligence, education, taste, and style mixed together so that you don't need any of those things. Good manners have a number of distinctive qualities: First, they can be learned by rote. This is a good thing; otherwise most rich men's daughters could not be displayed in public. Secondly, manners do not vary from culture to culture or place to place. The same polite behavior that makes you a welcome guest in the drawing rooms of Kensington is equally appropriate among the Mud People of the fierce Orokaiva tribe of Papua New Guinea—if you have a gun. This is the advantage of Western-style manners. Citizens of westernized countries still have most of the guns.

Another distinctive quality of manners is that they have nothing to do with what you do, only how you do it. For example, Karl Marx was always polite in the British Museum. He was courteous to the staff, never read with his hat on, and didn't make lip farts when he came across passages in Hegel with which he disagreed. Despite the fact that his political exhortations have caused the deaths of millions, he is today more revered than not. On the other hand, John W. Hinckley, Jr., was only rude once, to a retired Hollywood movie actor, and Hinckley will be in a mental institution for the rest of his life.

## HOW DO GOOD MANNERS WORK?

Manners exist because they are useful. In fact, good manners are so useful that with them you can replace most of the things lacking in modern life.

Good manners can replace religious beliefs. In the Episcopal Church they already have. Etiquette (and quiet, well-cut clothing) is devoutly worshipped by Episcopalians.

Good manners can replace morals. It may be years before anyone knows if what you are doing is right. But if what you are doing is nice, it will be immediately evident. Senator Edward Kennedy, for instance, may or may not be a moral person, but he is certainly a polite one. When Miss Kopechne seemed to be in trouble, Senator Kennedy swam all the way to Edgartown rather than run up a stranger's phone bill calling for help. You should be the same way yourself. If you happen to be on a sinking ship with too few lifeboats, take one and slip quietly away. There's going to be a terrific fuss among the drowning passengers, and it's rude to deliberately overhear an argument which is none of your concern.

Good manners can also replace love. Most people would rather be treated courteously than loved, if they really thought about it. Consider how few knifings and shootings are the result of etiquette as compared to passion.

And good manners can replace intellect by providing a set of memorized responses to almost every situation in life. Memorized responses eliminate the need for thought. Thought is not a very worthwhile pastime anyway. Thinking allows the brain, an inert and mushy organ, to exert unfair domination over more sturdy and active body parts such as the muscles, the digestive system, and other parts of the body you can have a lot of thoughtless fun with. Thinking also leads to theories, and theoretical correctness is always the antithesis of social correctness. How much better history would have turned out if the Nazis had been socially correct instead of true to their hideous theories. They never would have shipped all those people to concentration camps in boxcars. They would have sent limousines to pick them up.

Thinking is actually rude in and of itself. Manners involve interaction with others. You cannot, for instance, think and listen to what other people are saying at the same time. And what most people have to say doesn't merit much thought; so if you *are* caught thinking, you really have no excuse.

As a result of thinking's innate rudeness, thinking people are not often popular. Although the Curies were extremely famous, they were rarely invited out socially. They were too thoughtful. Also, they glowed.

The fact that good manners require interaction is finally their most useful trait. Manners force us to pay attention to the needs, desires, and hopes of other people. If you have good manners you will never become narcissistic and self-obsessed. A self-obsessed person is to be pitied; there are so many interesting people in the world, and while he's not paying attention to them, they will probably rob and cheat him.

# 2

# Creating a Persona: The Polite You

*How dreary to be somebody!*
*How public, like a frog*
*To tell your name the livelong June*
*To an admiring bog!*

— Emily Dickinson

*I*n order to know how to act, you must first know who you are. Very few people know who they are. And small wonder, since most people aren't anybody at all.

You, for instance, are probably no one in particular. This is because of your dull family. Boring people with humdrum

7

backgrounds were bound to raise a very ordinary you. A compelling persona is inherited. Our behavior is determined by our ancestors.

This is a grim statement and, fortunately, a false one. If our behavior were really determined by our ancestors, we'd all act like amoebas. We'd eat by osmosis and reproduce by division, meaning we'd smear food all over our bodies at dinner and have sex by throwing ourselves under a train.

In truth, it is no more necessary to go through life with the family you were born into than it is to wear diapers to your debutante ball. You can modify your family to suit your need for an interesting background and alter all your relatives so that you will inherit a fascinating personality from them. You can do this by the simple expedient of lying. Thank God, manners have nothing to do with facts.

## YOUR NEW FAMILY

Accompanying this chapter is a family tree you can adopt as your own. This genealogical history will give dignity to a rich person, breeding to a poor one, and, if used with wit and style, will make even a middle-class person socially acceptable.

Read the instructions carefully. Practice on sympathetic strangers. By the time you get done telling lies about who you are, you will have learned the truth about how you should act.

## HOW TO USE YOUR NEW FAMILY

To produce a truly interesting you, your ancestors should be varied and colorful types. The ten most important of these types are:

1. Exotic
2. Blue-blooded
3. Famous
4. Tainted with an Awful Secret
5. Venerable
6. Artistic
7. Sinful
8. Rich
9. Bad
10. Trendy

The attached genealogical chart provides you with one of each plus three optional subtypes: Mysterious, Crazy, and Tragically Dead.

**1. Princess Dog Feather**—*A Carib Indian, one of the few survivors of that nearly extinct tribe.*

A seafaring member of your family married her on the island of Dominica and brought her back to Massachusetts. The local rumor was that she never fully abandoned her native cannibalism. Indeed, a number of neighborhood children did disappear. But the New Bedford authorities were never able to prove anything.

Exotic ancestors are mostly good for cocktail-party small-talk. But you can also use them to explain cheap jewelry or an ill-conceived hairstyle. They will also go a long way toward excusing a bad accent if you have the nerve to claim some Carib was still spoken in your childhood home.

### 2. Lord Charles Hogford—*younger son of Viscount Uttershire and later Duke of Ohio.*

The more democratic a society becomes, the more people swoon for a title. Otherwise the Earl of Lichfield would be dragging a pony and an old Speed Graphic through the suburbs of Liverpool, taking toddler snaps. Unfortunately, there are only two ways for an American to get a title: either marry one (if you're a woman) or be made a papal count (if you're a man and a Catholic and a total humbug). Therefore you have to invent something. Let it drop that if Cornwallis hadn't been such a wimp at Yorktown, you might have a ducal estate in downtown Akron today. But don't overplay your hand. Universal love of titles is matched by universal hatred of inherited social status. Make your noble progenitor a debt-plagued wastrel. Say he was exiled to America and George II created him Duke of Ohio in hopes that he would go to that distant place and never find his way home.

### 3. Senator Henry Clay

Fame is even more valuable than nobility. And its standards are lower. In fact, there are none. A very quiet and tasteful way to be famous is to have a famous relative. Then you can not only be nothing, you can do nothing, too. This is the Alice Roosevelt Longworth kind of fame.

Anyway, pick a famous ancestor who's obscure enough and dead enough so you won't be caught out. And don't brag about him. You should deprecate his character just as you should deprecate your own. Remember the wisdom of Dr. Johnson, who said, "All censure of a man's self is oblique praise. It is in order to shew how much he can spare." Point out that Henry

Clay helped to provoke the stupid War of 1812, threw a fix into the election of John Quincy Adams, and, by his authorship of the Missouri Compromise, proved himself a poltroon on the slavery question.

**4. Marcus Aurelius Jackson**—*born a slave, later the wealthiest barber in Cairo, Illinois.*

Nothing makes an Awful Secret like a secret Negro. A secret like this allows you to act moody, resentful, guilty, depressed—in other words, allows you to act like everyone else, except *you* have an excuse. It's also great for seduction, especially down South. Tearfully confess that your family has been hiding this for a hundred and fifty years. The object of your desire will reciprocate immediately. *All* southern families have been hiding something for a hundred and fifty years. And nothing sparks an affair like shared paranoid psychosis. Up North, confess your bloodline freely. There's nothing a northerner likes better than a black person who is completely white. Do not, however, try this trick with real blacks. They could give a shit.

Incidentally, if you happen to *be* black, this relative will explain your color, and you can still have all the white ancestors, too. American blacks carry a lot more patrician blood in their veins than the sheet-draped yahoos who want to chase them off school buses.

(If you travel in very sophisticated circles, you may want to turn Marcus Aurelius into Moses Schmeckle. Racism is very lower-class. Upper-class people are never racists; they're anti-Semites.)

**5. Luther Burbank [your last name]**—*grandfather on your father's side.*

It's important to have someone intelligent, educated, and morally outstanding in the family. It impresses potential in-laws and gives your lawyer something to work with when he's trying to get you sentenced to a minimum-security federal tennis prison. Make Grandfather Luther a graduate of Stanford (Harvard is too obvious), and make his accomplishment just slightly silly so you can pass the information along with the right lightness of tone. Say he was a chemist and developed 106 industrial uses for lima-bean oil.

**6. Olive Oradell Entwhistle**—*grandmother on your father's side.*

Every fine family is leavened with a little bit of the artistic—emphasis on the little bit. The stock artist character is an amateur thespian and great beauty whose father would not allow her to go on the stage professionally. This is good if you're a Hollywood type. You can tell how Grandmother ran away to appear with the young Will Rogers in the Ziegfeld Follies and how Great-Grandfather followed her to New York and walked out of the audience right up onto the stage in the middle of a chorus number, grabbed her by the arm, and took her home.

But if you aspire to more elevated levels of society, make Grandmother a New England poet (intimate of the Lowells), who never published, and whose best work was destroyed by her mother for fear of scandal. A few poems survived, however, and were given to you when Grandma was on her deathbed. Use the love poems of Robert Herrick; no one has read those in a hundred years. Write them out in lavender ink on good stationery and leave the sheets in the sun for a month.

## Your New Family Tree

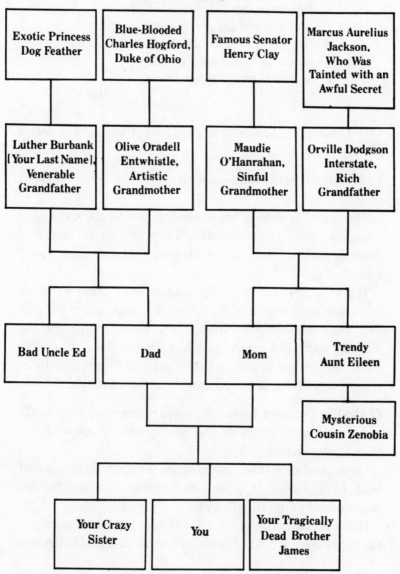

*Have ye beheld, with much delight,*
*A red rose peeping through a white?*
*Or ever marked the pretty beam*
*A strawberry shows, half drowned in cream?*
*So like to this, nay all the rest,*
*Is each neat niplet of her breast.*

*—O.O.E.*

Very authentic. And almost as good for getting laid as a secret Negro.

**7. Maudie O'Hanrahan**—*grandmother on your mother's side.*

The sins of yesterday are always enjoyed by the virtuous of today. So make Grandmother O'Hanrahan an old-fashioned *dame de plaisir*. This will give her—and, by extension, you— a heart of gold.

Tell your liberal friends about Grandma's angry views on the whole male sex—and capitalism and imperialism besides. Tell your conservative friends she never regretted her naughty youth and carried a lock of King Victor Emmanuel's pubic hair to her grave. It is the essence of courtesy to be sympathetic to the largest possible number of people.

**8. Orville Dodgson Interstate**—*grandfather on your mother's side, asphalt magnate and paving czar for whom Interstate 80 was named.*

No one will ever take your abilities seriously if there hasn't been some money in your family somewhere. People are suspicious of unrewarded virtue.

If you aren't rich, say Grandpa Orville lost all his money in the depression of 1921. It's a much more fashionable depression than the one in 1929. If you *are* rich, emphasize what a robber baron Grandpa was. Tell how he introduced anthrax into livery stables to boost the automobile trade and how he dug up paupers' graves to get the calcium for blacktop manufacture. People are also suspicious of *rewarded* virtue.

**9. Ed**—*your father's younger brother.*

He robbed a garage in Des Moines, lined up all the employees under a grease rack, and lowered an Oldsmobile on them.

It's nice to have someone who is really bad (as opposed to "sinful") in the family. It will make people think twice before they cross you in a business deal.

Ed is also valuable if you want to affect the left-wing opinions which are periodically fashionable among the over-educated. Turn the tables on Ed and Grandpa Luther and show how Ed was really performing an act of lumpen-proletariat revolutionary violence while Grandpa's supposed virtue only postponed the inevitable heightening of class contradictions or whatever it is that pinky-brains say these days.

**10. Eileen**—*your mother's older sister.*

She has lived in Paris for fifty years and was close friends with Faulkner, Tristan Tzara, Dorothy Parker, and anyone else from the twentieth-century hip scene whose name you'd like to drop. (In the popular imagination everyone from D. H. Lawrence to Thelonious Monk lived together in a big motel room in downtown Paris from 1920 until the war in Vietnam.) Eileen was involved in some terrible impropriety in whereveryou're-from. Mom will not speak her name. She smokes opium and has Arab boy "companions."

### 11. Mom and Dad

There's not much you can do with them. Try to give them an interesting past to make up for the dreary present. But remember to make the stories you tell about them the kind of stories they would be expected to deny. For instance, you can say that they abused you sexually. (A claim of sexual abuse by a parent is also sufficient to excuse everything you do for the rest of your life.)

## Optional Relatives

Caution: Be sure you live far enough (both socially and geographically) from where you were born to get away with imaginary immediate family members.

### 12. Cousin Zenobia—*illegitimate daughter (or son) of your Aunt Eileen.*

This one's strictly for fun. She (or he) took your virginity when you were twelve. Now she's (he's) a spy for the Mossad but possibly a PLO double-agent. She (he) will add considerable spice to your stories about the European package tour.

### 13. Jane—*your Moonie/est-nut/Jesus freak/et cetera sister.*

Every well-off family in America has a kid like this, and it would be inconsiderate of you not to have one in your family. Tell how your father tried to have her deprogrammed and after twenty-eight hours in a motel room Jane had converted a lawyer, two private detectives, and your mom.

## WHAT TO DO ABOUT THAT NAME

There's a long tradition of silly names in polite society: Sir John Suckling, Millard Fillmore, Algernon Swinburne, Beerbohm Tree, Armand Hammer, Pia Zadora, and so on. It's best to keep your own name even if it's awful. Brazen it out like an Englishman would. And if anyone laughs, punch him like an American.

It can even be an advantage to have a silly name if you're going into show business or such related fields as law and politics. If you don't have a bad name already, give yourself a terrible nickname. "Dirty," "Buggo," "Weenie," and "Blimp" are good. They'll make you "a character." And "a character" can get away with murder or, anyway, perjury, as "Tricky" Dick Nixon did.

Still, it's hard to be the right sort of person if you're called Clement Squid or something. But this is easy to fix.

An objectionable first name like "Rufus," "Melvin," "Eustace," or "Gladys" can become an initial or two. Thus the rather odd "Ignatius Aloysius Conners" becomes the perfectly normal "I.A. Conners." Add a third initial from some family name for extra pizzazz: "I.A.J. Conners."

A dull last name can be improved by using your mother's maiden name. "Bob Smith" will never be remembered by anyone and looks like adultery when you sign a hotel register. But "Williams Smith" is very nice.

Some ethnic groups, notably central Europeans,

have last names which sound very unfortunate in English. The usual approach is to shorten them. This wouldn't work with "Schlumfuch" or "Lipbum," however. So an alternate strategy is to add ethnically compatible syllables. "Schlumerfuchenstein" or "Lipperbummenman" are almost ridiculous enough to make you a Hapsburg prince.

The most difficult last names are the simply foolish, e.g., "Fink," "Nerts," "Stinkum," or "Balls," and those which require constant explanation, e.g., "Hitler" or "Mussolini." The trick here is to change the spelling and pronunciation in a small and natural way. There's nothing wrong with "Frank," "Neff," "Stankan," "Balsum," "Hittner," or "Mussoli."

Try to be reasonably honest with your name change. It shouldn't look as though you're trying to pull something. "Nowakowski" can become "Nowak" but not "Norwalk." "Pushkinikoff" can become "Pushkin" but not "Perkins." And use some logical occasion for your change of name—going away to school, for instance, or enlisting in the Army or having your first business card or by-line printed. Don't be shy about this. Ladies' man Gary Hartpence went so far as to run for President in order to have occasion to change his last name.

14. James—*your older brother (deceased).*

If you want to be excused for all sorts of terrible behavior and don't have the heart to claim that your parents molested you, then tell how you suffered awful emotional trauma because of James. He was everything your parents ever wanted in a child—handsome, smart, polite, popular, good at sports, and already accepted at Princeton in his junior year of high school. Then he stepped on a rusty croquet wicket and died from an allergic reaction to the tetanus shot. Of course you were never able to live up to his example.

Tell your friends that James used to torture animals and burgle neighborhood homes. But you've protected your parents from this knowledge all these years.

## REAL FAMILIES—WHICH SORT IS BEST?

To become a mannerly and courteous person you want only a few things from your real family: dignity, breeding, and piles of money. That's all anyone has ever wanted from a family. But all anyone gets from most families is love. And family love has nothing to do with "true love." Family love is messy, clinging, and of an annoying and repetitive pattern, like bad wallpaper.

### Are Rich Families Better?

Not necessarily and especially not in America. The dignity evaporates when you discover they made their fortune in dog laxatives.

As for breeding, most rich people are too busy getting divorced and drinking to have time to show their sons how to tie a Windsor knot or tell their daughters never to marry a man with that knot in his tie. Rich children are shipped to boarding schools, often before they are weaned. It would be unfair to call the atmosphere in these schools bestial. A child who was kept in the Bronx Zoo for twelve years would acquire more courtesy and taste. Occasionally boarding schools do turn out someone along the lines of the "preppy" stereotype. But in real life their graduates are more likely to wind up playing electronic xylophone, and singing 50s toothpaste commercials in a performance art ensemble.

And, when it comes to money, wealth does not guarantee it. Rich parents are famous both for miserliness and astonishing longevity. And, when they finally do die, you'll find they've left their estate in inviolate trust to the golden retrievers.

## Are Poor Families Any Improvement?

Poor families are much better. Of course, a poor family won't give you breeding, but it will give you preparation for life. It's far more instructive to have a drunk parent right there in the tenement with you than it is to have a drunk parent off in Gstaad. Poor families also scream at each other, never have spending money, and are prone to violence. This is excellent preparation for becoming, say, president of a large corporation—what with acrimonious board meetings, constant cash-flow problems, and corporate products that maim and kill people. In fact, being poor is generally much better for getting rich than being rich is. Poor people have a lot of time on their hands and spend it thinking up inexpensive and easily marketed fads like crack.

There is also dignity in being poor. A poor person who has made even slightly good is more admired than a rich person who has been only slightly bad. We are, after all, a nation of immigrants, laborers, common men. In our popular mythology, the lower classes are decent, hardworking, and possessed of simple piety and common sense—as long as they stay downwind. Your proletarian dignity, however, will do no good when your alcoholic bag lady mother comes looking for you in Four Seasons.

## What About Middle-Class Families?

Most of us don't have the luck to be either rich or poor. We are stuck, instead, with being embarrassed. There's tiresome Dad with his mailman shoes and his job selling wholesale something, and out-of-it Mom with her Mrs. George Bush hair and the pseudocolonial ranch in Dayton Acres with a Chevrolet Celebrity in the attached garage. The only possible thing you can do with a family like this is kill them. You'll probably get out of the mental hospital in five or six years, and when you do there'll be a fat book contract waiting. Tell your ghostwriter, "I did it because of the pole lamps." Every sensitive person will understand.

# 3

# The Fundamentals of Contemporary Courtesy

*Good breeding consists in concealing how much we think of ourselves and how little we think of the other person.*

—Samuel Clemens

The purpose of old-fashioned manners was to avoid attracting attention. The reason for this was that old-fashioned manners were possessed by only a few hundred rich people. These few hundred rich people didn't want all the hundreds of millions of poor people to notice who had the money. If the rich, polite few started attracting attention, the poor, rude many might get together and commit mayhem the way they did in Russia. The heck with that, said rich people.

But nowadays there are hundreds of millions of rich people, and poor people have been pretty much rendered harmless by drugs and sleeping on sidewalks. Plus it's getting so you can't tell rich from poor anyway, what with Nigerian illegal immigrants selling Rolexes on street corners and Gloria Vanderbilt putting her name on blue jean behinds. The problem modern people have is trying to be special. Therefore, the purpose of modern manners is to attract as much attention as possible.

## GREETINGS

The importance of conspicuousness in modern life has led to the phenomenon of "greeting inflation." Once, even the closest friends greeted each other with a polite bow. Today such reticence is almost extinct. A loud "Sweetheart," a slap on the back, chuck on the arm, tousling of hair, and a cheerful "Have a nice day!" will do if you don't know a person at all. But if you have even the slightest acquaintance with someone, it is usual to embrace him physically no matter what the circumstances. If you're carrying a briefcase or package, just throw it into the gutter. This makes a dramatic gesture of good fellowship.

If you actually know someone's name, twin kisses on both cheeks are expected and should be accompanied by some highly original term of endearment. "I love you" or "You're my best friend" isn't nearly strong enough. In California, where manners are more modern than anywhere else, people say, "I'd murder my parents to have lunch with you" or even "I'm so glad to see you that I'm going to give you gross points in my new movie." (The latter statement is a lie, by the way.)

## REBUFFS

At one time there was not only an etiquette of greeting people but also an etiquette of not greeting them. This ranged in degree from the coldly formal bow to the "cut direct." The cut direct was delivered by looking right at a person and not acknowledging his acquaintance or even his existence. This is no longer done. It has been replaced by the lawsuit. Opposing parties in a lawsuit (and other enemies) are expected to greet each other like lovers—especially now when it's so fashionable for hostesses to invite people who hate each other to the same dinners. If the enmity is minor or philosophical in nature, argument—or, better, tableware throwing—may resume after a drink or two. But if the hatred is deep and well occasioned, the mutual detestors are expected to chat amicably throughout the evening.*

## HAT, CANE, AND GLOVES

What to do with your hat and cane is a perennial awkwardness when greeting people. If the cane is necessary, it should

---

*See Chapter 5 for an explanation of this interesting custom.

be replaced with a crutch, which will gain you much more sympathy.

A hat should be taken off when you greet a lady and left off for the rest of your life. Nothing looks more stupid than a hat. When you put on a hat you are surrendering to the same urge that makes children wear mouse ears at Disney World or drunks wear lampshades at parties. Wearing a hat implies that you are bald if you are a man and that your hair is dirty if you are a woman. Every style of hat is identified with some form of undesirable (derby = corrupt ward heeler; fedora = male model; top hat = rich bum; pillbox = Kennedy wife, et cetera). Furthermore, the head is symbolically identified with the sexual organs, so that when you walk down the street wearing a hat, anyone who has the least knowledge of psychology will see you as having . . . a problem. A hat should only be worn if you are employed as a baseball player or are hunting ducks in the rain.

Gloves present another problem, especially when shaking hands. Men must always remove their gloves before a handshake. There is a good reason for this. A man can be very accurately judged by his hand. A soft hand indicates a lazy, unemployed person. A hard, calloused hand shows that a person is an ignorant and dull manual laborer. A cold, clammy hand means that a person is guilty and nervous. And a warm, dry hand means a person is incapable of feeling guilt and has the nerve to pull anything on you. A woman never removes her gloves. There's a good reason for this, too. A woman can also be very accurately judged by her hand, and why would she want to be?

## THE HANDSHAKE

Despite the popularity of more effusive forms of greeting, the handshake is omnipresent. It is now extended to everyone—men, women, old people, young children, and, especially, pet dogs.

It's important to develop a limp and affected handshake. A firm, hearty handshake gives a good first impression, and you'll never be forgiven if you don't live up to it. Also, a firm, hearty handshake inspires confidence in others. People who go around inspiring confidence in others are probably looking to sell them something. You don't want to appear to be that sort.

## FAREWELLS

Much more important than greeting people is saying good-bye to them or getting them to say good-bye to you or getting rid of them somehow anyway. The one thing that can be safely said about the great majority of people is that we don't want them around. Be sincere and forthright about the problem. Take the person you want to get rid of aside and tell him he has to leave because the people you're with hate him. Say, "I'm sorry, Fred, but you can't sit down with us. Molly and Bill Dinnersworth hate you because you're so much smarter and more successful than they are."

This is nasty and flattering at the same time. And it makes life more interesting, which, if you're too sophisticated to just want attention, is the point of existence.

## IN PUBLIC

If you don't manage to get rid of everyone and end up having to go somewhere with a group of people, make sure the couples are separated and that each partner is escorted by somebody new. This will give everyone something different to fight about later.

Generally speaking, a man is supposed to walk to the left of a woman and also keep himself between her and the curb. Of course, it is frequently impossible to do both. But the great thinkers of all ages have been unanimous in their admiration of paradoxes.

Unless he is helping her into an ambulance or a paddy wagon, a man is never supposed to touch a woman in public. That is, he shouldn't if he's married to the woman. Nothing is more deleterious to the spirit of romance than watching a married couple hold hands.

If a man is walking down the street with two women, he should keep them both on his right and not appear between them like an acrobat taking a bow. Every authority on etiquette mentions this precept. But what no authority on etiquette mentions is how a man can manage to get two women in the first place. The best idea is for him to convince his wife or girlfriend to talk a friend of hers into a threesome. Most likely the result will be physically and emotionally disastrous. But everyone will get something juicy to tell the psychiatrist and something to romanticize in diary or memoirs. Again, life is made more interesting.

It's no longer *de rigueur* for a man to burden himself with anything heavy that a woman is carrying, especially not a mortgage or someone else's baby. Nor should a man necessarily hold a door for a woman, unless it is a revolving door. It's not good manners to hold a revolving door, but it is lots of fun when other people are trapped inside.

## RESTAURANTS, TAXICABS, AND THE THEATER

When entering a restaurant, a man should allow the woman to precede him to their seats. This lets her find a friend whose table she can stand at and chat for half an hour while the man gets a chance to glimpse the prices on the menu and has a clear shot to bolt for the door when he sees those prices.

A wise woman allows a man to enter a taxicab ahead of her so she can slam his hand in the door if he's been acting like an ass.

At the theater, concert, or ballet, a man allows a woman to take her seat first. He then holds her coat on his lap, along with his own coat, her purse, her umbrella, both programs, and any other personal effects. Safely hidden behind this mound of belongings, he can go to sleep.

## THE IMPORTANCE OF BEING ON TIME

Whatever type of event you're attending, it's important to be on time. Being on time should not be confused with being prompt. Being prompt means arriving at the beginning. Being on time means arriving at the most interesting moment. Excepting love affairs, that moment is rarely the beginning.

"On time" is between midnight and four A.M. in New York, even for an eight o'clock play. Between midnight and four A.M. the actors will be getting drunk in a bar, and they'll be much more fun to talk to than when they're up on the stage.

In most other urban areas, "on time" is between twenty minutes and an hour late. This gives everyone else time to be late, too, and they'll appreciate it.

In the country being on time more nearly approximates being prompt. But don't overdo it. Being early is an unpardonable sin. If you are early, you'll witness the last-minute confusion and panic that always attend making anything seem effortlessly gracious.

In California, "on time" doesn't mean anything at all. An appointment for a meeting at three o'clock on Tuesday indicates there won't be a meeting and there might not be a Tuesday. Few words and no numbers have any meaning west of the Nevada border.

## AT HOME

One popular way to avoid the problem of being on time is to stay at home and conduct your life over the telephone. This is very chic in New York. Even New Yorkers who occasionally go outdoors have taken to telephoning every person they know once a day and twice if any of them has anything awful to say about the others.

Living over the telephone has a number of advantages. It saves on cab fare and clothing budgets, and love affairs can be conducted without the bother of contraception or hairdressers. In fact, with judicious use of answering machines, a love affair can be conducted without the bother of ever talking to the loved one.

## MAKING UP IN PUBLIC

It's bad manners to apply cosmetics in public. It reminds people that you need them.

---

### CODE OF A MODERN GENTLEMAN

1. Never strike anyone so old, small, or weak that verbal abuse would have sufficed.
2. Never steal anything so small that you'll have to go to an unpleasant city jail for it instead of a minimum security federal tennis prison.
3. Remember, the truth is rude. Consider the truth about where babies come from, especially some people's.
4. Never be unfaithful to a lover, except with your wife.
5. Never transmit a sexual disease in public.
6. Women and children should be protected in every tax-deductible way.
7. Don't pull on a crewneck sweater with a lit cigarette in your mouth.

---

## SMOKING IN PUBLIC

Smoking was once subject to all sorts of polite restrictions, but now it's just illegal. Therefore, there's only one remaining rule of etiquette about smoking in public: make sure you don't smoke anywhere else. Smoking is an inexpensive and convenient means of showing fashionable contempt for middle-class rules and regulations. Smoking also looks good. People who don't smoke have a terrible time finding something polite to do with their lips. But, when no one's around to see you, it doesn't matter what you do so there's no point in smoking then.

If someone asks you not to smoke, tell him you have no intentions of living to be an embittered old person. But thank him for his concern.

## NONCHALANCE

Nonchalance about health and well-being is what gives smoking its charm. That same nonchalance is at the heart of all really good manners. The most fundamental lesson of etiquette is "be unconcerned." Proper behavior means always giving the appearance of unperturbed grace. This appearance is much easier to achieve if you really *don't* care about anything. And this is why people always seem to be on their best behavior right before they commit suicide.

# 4

# *Important People: When to Stand Up, When to Sit Down, and When to Roll Over and Play Dead*

*Of beasts, it is confess'd, the ape,*
*Comes nearest us in human shape;*
*Like man he imitates each fashion,*
*And malice is his ruling passion;*
*But both in malice and grimaces,*
*A courtier any ape surpasses.*
                              —Oliver Goldsmith

$\mathcal{A}$n important person should be treated exactly like anyone else holding a gun at your head.

Fortunately there aren't many important people. To be important a person must be able to have an effect on your life. But the anarchy, entropy, and confusion in what's left of Western civilization make it difficult for anyone to have any effect on anything. Therefore this chapter is about people who are *called* important rather than people who *are* important. The headwaiter at Ma Maison, IRS auditors, and your immediate superior at work are important enough to be treated under separate headings.

## PEOPLE WHO ARE IMPORTANT "TO ME"

Some people who are called important are the "to me" kind of important, as in "My parents are important to me." If it is necessary to explain that someone is important to you, that explanation is all you are socially obligated to do for him. He isn't that important.

## FAMOUS PEOPLE

Other people who are called important are actually famous. Of course, they aren't important, either. And it would be hard to think of anything less important than some of them. A lamprey is more important than Bianca Jagger. But it is not a lie to call famous people important, because it isn't they to whom we are referring. It's their fame. Fame is very important. Modern society is without any concept of dignity, worth, or regard. Today the only thing which sets one person apart from another is his or her degree of fame.

Social obligations to the modern or famous type of important people are enormous and complex. We must be as obsequious as possible to famous people and do everything in our power to make them like us. Fame is a communicable disease. And if you kiss the ass of someone who's got it, you may catch it yourself.

## INTRODUCTIONS

In order to meet famous people and give them the opportunity to take advantage of you, an introduction is necessary. Asking for their autograph or running up to their restaurant table and gushing over their latest cause for notoriety ("I *loved* your divorce!") won't do.

The perfectly correct and most formal introduction is: "Mr. Awfulpics, may I present Mr. Climby" or "Mr. Grosspoints, may I present you to Miss Bedable." Or use the word "introduce" instead of "present." It's almost as correct and not as stupid sounding. The less famous person is presented to the more famous person. But men are always presented to women no matter how many times the man has appeared on the cover of *Time* and no matter how obvious it is that the woman wants to sleep with him just because he has. The only circumstance in which a woman is presented to a man is if that man is President of the United States—and who'd want to sleep with *him*?

## CHILDREN

Children are never introduced at all unless the famous person has a thing for them and you have one paid for and ready at the time.

## SUBFAMOUS PEOPLE

Of course, the very formal method of introduction is never used by sophisticated people because sophisticated people have never had occasion to read a book of etiquette. Besides, most of them know each other already. But it is wise to use the most ceremonious forms with people such as game-show hosts, rock-star wives, daytime television personalities, Cher's boyfriends, and others who might be insecure about their social status because they have none.

Otherwise, introductions are tailored to the circumstances and to the amount of fame involved. If there is no fame involved and you're just introducing one worthless friend of yours to another, you can say simply, "Don't you guys know each other?" and walk away.

## INSIGNIFICANT FRIENDS

When you want to introduce an insignificant friend to a famous person, you probably don't really *want* to at all. It's hard to do what you really want all the time, but, like every difficult task, it results in a feeling of great accomplishment and satisfaction. Just leave your friend standing there like furniture while you chat happily with the MTV veejay, mafia hit man, or elected official.

If you owe money to the friend or are married to him or her and taking this tack will get you in trouble, you can say, "Oh, by the way, Mr. Panflash, this is Alice. We went to the same child psychiatrist back in Lake Forest." If you have an ancient acquaintance with someone not worth knowing, most people will at least pretend to forgive you—the way they would pretend to forgive you for a birth defect or the wrong racial background. Of course, your spouse—whom you met two weeks ago in a health club—may be perplexed by this explanation, but that's what your spouse gets for trying to marry up.

## AMBITIOUS FRIENDS

Introducing an ambitious friend to a famous person is more tricky. It's not done unless the friend is so ambitious that he might be of use to you someday. Ambitious people are a lot more annoying than worthless people. Strategically, you don't want to alienate the friend, but, tactically, you don't want to be remembered for foisting that friend on your famous acquaintance. Say, "Mrs. Greedagent, this is my friend Mark. He's involved in a lot of really interesting cable TV projects." You've used the phrase "cable TV projects"—international code words for "unemployed and on the make"—so the celebrity cannot claim she wasn't warned. Change "cable TV projects" to "video art" if you think it will be a really long, long time before your friend is famous himself.

## WHEN TWO PEOPLE ARE BOTH IMPORTANT

Introducing important people to each other is much more satisfying than introducing them to video artists. One approach is to do everything you can to make them attractive to each other and hope that you will receive a sort of social "finder's fee" if they hit it off. They won't. The social habits of famous people are like the sexual practices of porcupines, which urinate on each other to soften the quills. A more interesting thing to do is to make sure the two important people loathe each other right from the start: "Ana Plotless, this is Bret Leadpart. Bret thinks your novels are very good—of their kind. . . . Bret, Ana has told me that she's heard you're very famous—in Japan." This way you'll become the conduit for all sorts of wonderful maliciousness between these two august souls.

# WHEN ONE PERSON IS IMPORTANT AND THE OTHER PERSON IS "INTERESTING"

The most delightful introduction you can make is to introduce an important person to someone he or she is going to find sexually interesting. This introduction is made in two parts. First you prep the sex object: "Kiki, save the drugs for later. I'm going to introduce you to Antonio. Antonio is a famous photographer. . . . Yes, he does lots of fashion—Paris *Vogue*." Then you march Kiki over to your well-known friend. "Antonio, you're going to love this girl. She once made Warren Beatty bleed out the ears." Kiki's name is not a necessary part of the transaction.

# INTRODUCING YOURSELF

There is only one person you can never introduce to the famous and that is yourself. Therefore it's good to cultivate the affections of professional sycophants such as publicists, movie agents, and freelance writers for *Vanity Fair* magazine. These people are understandably short of friends, and, if you are kind to them, they'll let you get the benefit of celebrity acquaintance while they do the fawning and toadying necessary for such acquaintance to be achieved.

## MAKING FAMOUS PEOPLE
## COMFORTABLE

Once you've met a famous person, say something that will make you remembered: "Cornelia Guest! Oh, my gosh, Miss Guest, I know it's polite for a gentleman to remove his hat when he meets a lady, but for you, I feel I should do something more, like take off my pants!!!"

Then shut up. Famous people think they want to be treated like regular people. This is not true. Famous people also think they are special and wonderful. This is even less true. The best course of action is to go ahead and treat them as if they are ordinary (because, boy, are they ever) but now and then throw something into the conversation to show that you share their completely wrong-headed opinion of their own wonderfulness: "Gosh, Cornelia, you make liposuction *come alive!*"

When the famous person you've met is not in your immediate company, ignore him or her completely. This is the modern use of the "cut direct" mentioned in Chapter 3. Whereas, in former times, the cut direct was used on enemies, it has now evolved into a polite way to show respect for famous friends. It is an article of faith among celebrities that they are constantly pestered by the public. Of course there are so many celebrities, and so few of them are celebrated for anything, that most of the time the public can't be bothered. But it's only common courtesy to act as though the famous people you know are so famous that the public is very bothered indeed. You don't want to be seen as part of that public. Wait for the celebrities to pester you. They will soon enough. If they weren't infantile self-obsessed hogs for attention, then our kind of society never would have thought they were important in the first place.

# 5

# *Table Manners*

> *Put not another bit into your mouth till the*
>   *former be Swallowed.*
> *Cleanse not your teeth with the Table Cloth,*
>   *Napkin, or Fork or Knife.*
> *Spit not in the fire.*
> *Kill no Vermin as Flees, lice, ticks & cet. in the*
>   *Sight of Others.*
>
> —George Washington (age fifteen)
> "Rules of Civility"

*T*able manners are a test to
see whether you're acting like a beast because you're rudely
ignorant or acting like a beast because you're fashionably
amusing. Fashionably amusing table manners are a matter of
breaking the right rule at the right time.

## DINNER PARTIES—ARRIVAL

It isn't necessary to arrive at a dinner party any later than extremely late, as usual—unless you have acquired a scandalous new dress or a black eye from a famous lover or something else that demands an entrance. In that case it's incumbent upon you to arrive after everyone else is seated. A hostess will wait for a tardy guest: ten minutes for a man, fifteen minutes for a woman, and half an hour for someone with a scandalous new dress or a black eye from a famous lover. Do not apologize for being late, especially not in a timid or embarrassed manner. A show of rudeness is quickly forgotten, but a show of cowardice never is—especially not from a person in a dress like yours.

## BEING ANNOUNCED

If the dinner is being given by someone very rich or someone behaving with your tax dollars as if she were, you may be announced by the butler. Tell him a funny name to say, like "Mr. Hugh G. Rection," or mock him in a high voice. He says, "Mr. Funguest, Mrs. Funguest," and you say, "With their dog Jingo." (Jingo can eat at the table where the hostess seats her cousins and brother-in-law.)

# THE THREE STAGES OF A FORMAL DINNER PARTY

There are three stages to a formal dinner party: the stage at which no one can be convinced to go in and sit down, the stage at which no one can be convinced to get up and leave, and the stage at which everyone argues loudly through the centerpiece and gets food all over expensive clothes.

Part of the reluctance to sit down to dinner stems from the fact, mentioned in Chapter 3, that it's fashionable to invite intense personal enemies to the same meal. This makes the party "interesting." Whatever enemy of yours is invited, he or she will be seated next to you. This is not the person with whom you argue loudly. You and your enemy should act like best friends for the same reason that China and Russia act that way when the U.S. is watching. The nervous effect on your hostess will make the party interesting for you, too. The loud arguing should be done with a real best friend—in order to broaden your acquaintance. Frequent changes of friends and underwear are marks of sophistication centuries old.

## TABLE TALK

The proper subject of dinner-table conversation with people other than best friends is savage criticism of the food. This used to be considered poor form, but that was when food was better and so were people. Criticizing a hostess's food is now considered Christian charity compared to what you could be saying about the hostess herself.

## DINNER SERVICE

One of two kinds of service will be offered at the dinner table: either the *service russe* or the so-called "American service." In the *service russe*, the maid serves each guest individually while her boyfriend robs their cars. In American service, the maid brings in a dish which is served by the hostess, and the plates are passed around the table from guest to guest. This gives the maid time to go outside and help steal car stereos.

*Service russe* is thought to be more truly formal, and one of its rules is that the table is never bare. There is always a plate in front of each guest. Another rule, especially at political dinners, is that nothing on that plate should taste better than the plate itself. Each dish is divided into individual servings in the kitchen and served from a platter at the guest's left. The guest slips the serving spoon under a portion and, steadying it with the serving fork, transfers it to his or her plate. Wise guests are cautioned not to clown around while doing this. It's too apt to look as though you've never seen a servant before—unless you really have the ability to slap the bottom of the platter with your left hand, make a cutlet fly in the air, and skewer it with your dinner fork while yelling "Kangaroo meat!"

## CORRECT TABLE SETTINGS

Table settings do not matter to anyone sane. A person with very definite opinions about china patterns is liable to have opinions about everything, including politics and religion, and that is a sign of mental imbalance.

Tables themselves, however, matter greatly. No decent person has a glass-topped table. Glass-topped tables make strategic shin-kicks and knee fondling visible to everyone.

Place mats are also unacceptable for formal dinners. The table covering or bare tabletop (and the china and glassware, too) must be easily damageable. This lets the hostess seem rich enough to be cavalier about material possessions and lets the guests wreak expensive revenge on the hostess for her seating arrangements.

## "USING THE RIGHT FORK"

Many people, when faced with a formal dinner, worry about what utensil to use and when. Although "using the right fork" is almost synonymous with "good etiquette," the phrase is largely symbolic. Among fashionable people this is not really considered very important. If you actually don't know which thing to use for what, just start at the outside of the stuff lying around your plate and work inward, changing implements with every course. Stop when you get to the saltcellar, however, and don't use this to scoop up bites of sherbet. That's bound to look stupid.

If your hostess happens to be as ignorant as you are and has laid out the silverware all wrong, then just use common sense. Put each implement to the use for which it seems most suited. Never stab anyone with a gravy ladle. And don't clean your ears with the fish knife. That should be done with the handle of the demitasse spoon. Also, don't steal silver that matches your own pattern at home. This looks too calculating. If all else fails, look around, watch what others are doing, and do the same thing. This should make for a delightful evening of drunkenness, flirtations, loud pointless laughter, and ill-advised invitations to your country place.

## PROPER USE OF THE NAPKIN

More important than proper use of the silverware is proper use of the napkin. The best way to use a napkin is as a mantilla to imitate your grandmother in church while grace is being said or as a pretend matador's cape to wave at undercooked beef or as a bandana to cover your face when you pull a stickup on your dinner partner with a lamb-chop pistol and demand "a date for the movies next Saturday night or your life."

## NOISES MADE WHILE EATING

Another common table-manners worry is about making noise while you eat. There's nothing wrong with making noise while you eat, as long as it's the right kind of noise. The right kind of noise sounds like this: "You *did?* How fabulous! Oh, I *envy* you—honestly . . . She *didn't?* How awful! . . . I *couldn't* agree with you more. You did exactly the right thing, dear." Industrial noises, barnyard sounds, and the squeals and grunts of lovemaking, however, are considered out of place.

## TALKING WITH THE MOUTH FULL

Talking with the mouth full is all right. Everyone does it. But don't listen with the mouth empty. It looks too much as though you're paying close attention to what's being said. And if you do that, people won't say things they really shouldn't.

## MISCELLANEOUS DETAILS

Additional sources of confusion at formal dinners are the propriety of refusing what's served and the question of what the finger bowls are for. Take lots of whatever's offered. Then don't eat it. It's very chic not to eat, but refusing a dish interrupts the orderly balletic flow of service and alerts everyone at the table to the fact that you're fat. Especially do not refuse wine. It is an odd but universally held opinion that anyone who doesn't drink must be an alcoholic.

Finger bowls are there to keep the conversation going. Point out to your dinner companion that these "Protestant bidets" are not nearly large enough for the important kinds of washing.

## "RETIRING" AFTER DINNER

At the end of dinner it used to be that the men would retire to the billiard room and the women would go into the parlor. Men and women no longer separate after dinner, however.

They now separate after twenty years of apparently happy marriage.

## RESTAURANT MANNERS

The table manners you have in a restaurant are very different from those you have in the home of a friend because, in a restaurant, you're allowed to play with your food. If you eat enough expensive meals and drink enough expensive liquor in a restaurant, you're allowed to do anything. But in the home of a friend, no matter how much you eat and drink, it won't excuse you for "restoring" a Renoir with potatoes *au gratin*.

## PLAYING WITH FOOD

Playing with food is the main reason that dining in restaurants has become so popular. Playing with food is a psychologically powerful way of attracting attention to yourself. And restaurants are better places to attract attention than friends' homes are, anyway. You usually know who's going to be at a friend's home. But practically anybody could be at a restaurant. If you attract enough attention in a restaurant, maybe a rich, beautiful person will give you money and sex.

Playing with food is easy. There are so many wonderful props right at hand. Breathes there a man with soul so dead that he's immune to the theatrical possibilities of a plate full of fried calamari? Even bank presidents and Presbyterian ministers have been known to put the tentacle parts up their noses and pretend the garlic bread is Captain Nemo's submarine, *Nautilus*. But playing with food must be done exactly right or it will lead to social disaster.

The secret to successful sport with foodstuffs is correct attitude. Playing with food has to be fast, loud, and enthusiastic. You must make your high spirits contagious before anyone has time for second thoughts. Second thoughts always consist of calling the police.

But if your attitude and timing are right, you can put a lettuce-leaf lion's mane around the neck of your date, hold her at bay with your chair, command her to leap upon the table and rear up on her hind legs, and everyone will think it's great fun.

Here are some other things you can do:

• Use steamed mussels as castanets, slip sugar bowls over the toes of your shoes, and do a flamenco dance on your chair.

• If everyone is having beef dishes, run around the table and try to put the cow back together.

• Use any roast whole bird as a hand puppet. You can achieve remarkably realistic effects by jamming your thumb and forefinger into the wing sockets. Point out that the bird has lost its head, so it has no sense at all, which is why it's flying around the table squeezing people's noses.

• Illustrate Persian Gulf battle strategy on the napkin in someone's lap. Asparagus spears are capital ships; chunks of *boeuf bourguignon* are air-to-surface missiles, et cetera.

• Hang a grilled brook trout on the wall like a trophy, or, better, stand on the table and re-enact landing it with an umbrella and shoelace.

• Gather up veal scallops and have an impromptu game of cards—sauce Milanese is trump.

• Use a raw oyster to show someone what a French kiss would be like if she'd married a reptile.

The list is endless. Let imagination, rather than taste, be your guide.*

## FOOD FIGHTS

Food fights are unattractive events. They are messy, childish, and wasteful. No decent person ever starts a food fight he's not sure he can win.

The important thing in a food fight is weaponry. Forget bread rolls and sugar cubes. Linguine garrotes are much better, and nothing tops a stuffed pork chop hit with your shoe so that the dressing is projected across the room. The idea is to shock and terrify your adversary into submission. Go for something that will incapacitate his second-strike capabilities, such as a flipped spoonful of pears flambé or weapons of utter surprise such as porterhouse steak Frisbees.

A word of warning to the young: never have a food fight with school-dining-hall food. It's too dangerous. Once, a few years ago, at Phillips Exeter Academy, a student was hit in the face with a piece of dining-hall meatloaf. Some of it got in his mouth, and he died.

---

*Henry Beard, one of the founders of the *National Lampoon* magazine and America's premier living expert on playing with food, has a great stunt with stainless-steel hinged-top coffee creamers. Using his thumb to move the creamer lid, Henry gets "Carl the Creamer" to talk. Carl (he speaks in a very high voice) says, "Henry, I'm *hungry*." Henry feeds Carl all sorts of things—sugar packets, bits of squashed-up food, cigarette butts, and so on. But Carl always eats too much. "Henry, I feel sick," he says. Then Carl throws up on somebody at the table whom no one can stand.

# 6

## Acting Up

*The heart of the wise is in the house of*
*mourning: but the heart of fools is in the house*
*of mirth.*

—Ecclesiastes 7:4

$\mathcal{I}$t is a basic tenet of modern
manners that everyone likes to act up. There's nothing wrong
with this. But remember what we've said about table manners
and be sure you know which rules you're breaking. The only
unforgiveable acts of misbehavior are accidental. Ignorance of
the law is no defense and ignorance of the laws of etiquette is
a crime in itself.

If you throw a drink in the face of a congressman, it will be regarded as a political statement, or as a moral judgment, or as an enviable thing others had been dying to do. But *if you did not know* he was a congressman, it will be regarded as felonious assault.

## ACTING CUTE

Once you know what you're doing is wrong, it's easy to learn how to get away with it. The first technique of misbehavior is to be cute. When the generation born after World War II began to act up, they wore feathers in their hair, put paint on their noses, and went around sticking chrysanthemums down rifle barrels. *Life* magazine adored it—it was so cute. But later they began doing things which were much less cute, like threatening to vote, and it became necessary to kill them at Kent State. Of course, "hippies" were also violating a basic principle of cuteness; they were getting old. To be cute you must be young. If you had a great big adult dog and it whined all night, tore up your shoes, and messed on the rug, you'd have it gassed. But when a puppy does these things, it's cute.

## BEING RICH

If you can't be cute, be rich. Rich people are allowed to water stock issues, manipulate commodity prices, and trade bonds with privileged information gained on the squash court. The equivalent sorts of things, when done by poor people, are called stealing. The same double standard applies to a number of other activities such as operating motor vehicles under the influence of alcohol (as long as the motor vehicle is a yacht) and creating a public nuisance, like the IBM headquarters building in Manhattan. We allow a great deal of latitude to the rich. This is our way of making it up to them for creating a society in which everything can be had for money, but nothing is worth having.

## BEING PRETTY

Even better than being cute or rich is being pretty. Pretty people are forgiven absolutely anything they do. And there's a very good reason for it. If it weren't for them, masturbation would be so dull for the rest of us.

## BEING FULL OF CHARM

If you are adult, homely, and poor, the best you can do is be charming. Try to make the bad things you do fun for everyone. If you're drinking and driving and you smash into a car, give the other driver a drink, too, and be sure to offer one to the police when they arrive. This won't actually keep you out of trouble, but it does allow the festivities to continue a little longer and that's almost as good.

## BEING INSANE

If you lack charm, claim insanity. Being insane is excellent for getting away with silly behavior like throwing a chair at Geraldo Rivera. A good lawyer can probably get your jail sentence for assault reduced to a few psychiatric sessions—if public sentiment is on your side (that is, if you hurt Geraldo badly enough to keep him off the air). At psychiatric sessions you can do anything you want. Throw a chair at the psychiatrist, for example. Go ahead. It's considered therapeutic.

The only trouble with an insanity plea is that insanity has become so widespread lately that you may run across a judge who's just as crazy as you are. You could end up in something much worse than jail, such as a panel discussion of Satanism with Geraldo Rivera.

## PROPER USE OF SELF-DESTRUCTION

If none of this is working, turn the destruction on yourself. When you've been around the dance floor at the bachelor's cotillion cutting up people's clothing with pinking shears, don't forget to snip off your own lapels. When you're busting somebody's collection of Boehm china birds, bust them on your own forehead. It's people who live in *brick* houses who shouldn't throw stones. By hurting yourself you show others that what you're doing is "adorable," "extravagant," or "uncontrollable" not aggressive. This was the difference between Jim Jones in Guyana and Charles Manson in L.A., for instance. Sort of.

Speaking of suicide, that's a good ploy, too, if you've been very, very bad. With a little experimentation you'll find there are a dozen ways to cut yourself around the wrist area and bleed all over the place without real danger to anything but the carpet. Or, you don't have to do anything to yourself at all. Just call a friend and *say* you've taken a bottle of Nembutal. Everything will be forgiven. Of course, at the hospital they'll probably insist on pumping your stomach. But this will seem a small price to pay if you've checked to see what Boehm china birds are worth.

## PROPER USE OF CASH

Suicide is one way to pay for the destruction you've wrought, but there's nothing wrong with paying for it in actual money. Alas, if you've really had fun, full compensation will be way beyond your means. The easiest thing to do is carry a big roll of money with you wherever you go. This should consist of one fifty-dollar bill wrapped around about fifty ones. (Anybody should be willing to pay a hundred dollars for a really fabulous melee in which he starred as the center of attention.) Then—after you've upended your hostess's Hepplewhite chairs and piled them in the center of the room to reenact your great uncle's exploits at the siege of Lady-smith, and torn down your hostess's drapes to do your impression of Armani's fall line, and used two bottles of Beaujolais-Villages to show her how much better the Chinese rug would look in burgundy—*then* you can toss your roll on the hall table and swiftly bid *adieu*. You'll be long gone by the time she's counted it. And, later, when she tells everyone you didn't leave enough to cover damages, they'll just think she's trying to belittle your grand gesture.

## MISCHIEF THAT PAYS FOR ITSELF

It's only natural to want to avoid paying for the mischief you do, but trying to get mischief itself to pay is another matter and very bad manners unless you've been elected to Congress or hired by Drexel, Burnham, Lambert for that purpose.

## MAKING UP A GOOD EXCUSE

The very last and most desperate means of getting away with misbehavior is by making up an excuse. This is extremely risky. All the world hates an excuse. Also, an excuse only works when you have an audience that's very sympathetic to you in the first place, such as your mother. But sometimes you do something so bad—being a Nazi, for instance—that it demands *some* kind of excuse.

Here's an exercise in excuse making which illustrates some of the difficulties: Pretend you are Adolph Eichmann and you're trying to excuse yourself to your mother for having killed hundreds of thousands of Jews at Auschwitz. See if any of these excuses work:

- I was in a real rush and I just threw something together.
- Isn't that just like me? I could kick myself.
- I was under a lot of pressure at work.

# 7

# Drinking

*And malt does more than Milton can*
*To justify God's ways to man.*

—A. E. Housman

The only really courteous excuse for misbehavior is "I was drunk." No one will forgive you for doing terrible things because you were drunk, but that's not the point. "I was drunk" is a polite way of saying, "I shed my inhibitions and did exactly what I wanted to do, and if you provoke me, I'll do it again." This gives people fair warning and tells them tactfully to mind their own business.

But drinking is not really a matter of manners. It is a matter of necessity. Modern life would be unbearable without liquor.

## ALCOHOL AND YOUNG PEOPLE

Alcohol is very important for young people because it provides a sort of "liquid adulthood." If you are young and you drink a great deal it will spoil your health, slow your mind, make you fat—in other words, turn you into an adult. Also, if you want to get one of those great red beefy, impressive-looking faces that politicians and corporation presidents have, you had better start drinking early and stick with it. Drinking will also give you a mature and authoritative-sounding voice, especially when combined over a long period of time with lots of cigarettes.

## ALCOHOL AND MATURE ADULTS

If you are older, alcohol is even more important. It provides you with all those things which are lacking in modern life because of the disappearance of organized religion and domestic servants: Alcohol makes you feel important when you are not. If you *are* important, it makes you feel safe. Alcohol gives you an incontrovertible reason not to have sexual relations. And, what's best, alcohol provides that most difficult of all things for an adult to achieve, sleep. The single drawback to alcohol is that you might not drink enough of it and may consequently live so long you'll see all the things you've been dreading come to pass—greenhouse effect, 100% heterosexual AIDS virus exposure, nuclear war, and friends with machines on their telephones that not only answer calls but make them.

## MANNERS WHEN SOBER

There is a side to drinking that does have to do with courtesy, however. That is, there are times when it would be really bad manners to be sober. Some of these occasions are:

- Funeral of anyone you knew or claimed to
- Daughter's wedding reception
- Own wedding
- Anytime the Dow-Jones average drops more than 500 points in a day

Not to be drunk in these situations will make you look unfeeling, insensitive, and in the case of the last, financially inconsequential.

## REGURGITATION COURTESY

The part of drinking, though, where manners are really most involved is the part where you throw up.

Every authority on etiquette discusses how to put things into your stomach, but very few discuss how to get them back out in a hurry. Actually, there is no way to making vomiting courteous. You have to do the next best thing, which is to vomit in such a way that the story you tell about it later will be amusing. It's always good manners to provide entertainment.

The author himself can give an example from an incident that befell him when he was a young man at school. He was hosting a party and ran short of liquor at two A.M. He drove with some friends to the outskirts of the little college town and returned with moonshine whiskey. Everyone drank it; everyone began to vomit. The author, being a fastidious type, managed to crawl upstairs to the toilet, where he threw up and, at length, passed out.

In the morning he awoke with a remarkable headache, a sort of ring of pain all around his skull. At first he did not have the courage to open his eyes; the prospect of daylight was too painful. When he did finally peek out, however, he found there was nothing there. He opened his eyes wide, blinked them repeatedly, but, still, everything before him was blank. "Oh, God!" he thought, "I'm blind. Blind! I drank wood alcohol and I'm blind!" And he went on like that, in a state of panic, for nearly ten minutes before he realized he'd passed out with his head upside down in the toilet with the water up to his eyebrows, and all he could see was the porcelain bowl.

Another story which is frequently told is about a young man who is at a wedding and has too much to drink. He is overcome by a vivid realization that he is going to be sick *immediately*. There is no time to reach any sanitary facility. So he bolts to a window, sticks his head through, and vomits— only to realize a moment later that the wedding is taking place *outdoors*. This story is probably stolen from the first chapter of Evelyn Waugh's *Brideshead Revisited*. But that only makes it better. (Try not to be too original with your vomiting story or someone may make it into a movie comedy starring Dan Aykroyd and not credit you.)

A second important consideration of vomiting etiquette is to make sure what you throw up matches what your date is wearing. If your date is wearing white, stick to Chablis, potatoes, veal *piccata*, and so forth. If your date is wearing navy blue, it is much more difficult. There aren't that many blue foods. Go with dark colors—beef well-done, spinach salad, the heartier Burgundies. If you're attending a golf tournament, regatta, or other sporting event where everyone is wearing brightly colored resort clothes, you might want to try lima beans and Lancer's *vin rosé*.

Incidentally, this is why we drink red wine with red meat and white wine with poultry and fowl in the first place—so our vomit doesn't clash.

# 8

# *Taking Drugs*

*Death before dishonor.*
*Drugs before lunch.*
 —Motto of the Aspen Drug and Gun Club


*P*eople don't take drugs any-
more. Nobody in the United States ever takes an illegal drug
anymore, not even an occasional puff on a joint. All those
drugs we see all the time—those huge drug busts on the
evening news—that's just something the DEA cooks up to get
on television. Therefore this chapter on drug etiquette is
completely unnecessary. Skip it and go on to the next chapter.
The next chapter is about conversation. There are a lot of
useful hints and tips in the next chapter. Hints and tips about
lying through your teeth, for instance.

| PROPER SOCIAL BEHAVIOR UNDER THE INFLUENCE OF DRUGS | | | | | |
| --- | --- | --- | --- | --- | --- |
| DRUG | SOCIAL OCCA-SIONS APPRO-PRIATE TO USE | WHAT TO DO | WHAT TO SAY | WHAT TO BREAK | HOW TO EXCUSE YOUR-SELF THE NEXT DAY |
| Alcohol | Any | Shed clothes in restaurant, don dress belt with napkin draped over crotch, stand on chair and recite "Hia-watha" | "Where's the par-rrrrrr-rty!?" | Dishes, marriage vows | "I hadn't eaten anything since lunch." |
| Marijuana | Rock con-certs, hor-ror movie screen-ings, time spent alone in bedroom as a teen-ager | Listen to Guns and Roses on stereo, look at Bloom-ingdale's under-wear cata-logue, eat Mallomars | "Wow." "Oh, wow." "Really." "Wow." | Glass bongs, lava lamps | "Wow, that *sin-semilla* is really heavy shit." |

| PROPER SOCIAL BEHAVIOR UNDER THE INFLUENCE OF DRUGS | | | | |
|---|---|---|---|---|
| **DRUG** | **SOCIAL OCCASIONS APPROPRIATE TO USE** | **WHAT TO DO** | **WHAT TO SAY** | **WHAT TO BREAK** | **HOW TO EXCUSE YOURSELF THE NEXT DAY** |
| Cocaine | Visits to dance clubs and other moments of private desperation | Do more coke | Say you never do coke anymore | Promises | If you have any left, you'll still be there acting up. |
| LSD | College reunions, weekends in Big Sur | Stare at rocks, trees, bugs, self | "This is incredible! I forgot how incredible this is! Incredible! Really incredible!" | The space/time continuum | Freak out and cry |
| Crack | Robbery, burglary, assault, murder | Robbery, burglary, assault, murder | "Yo." | Laws | Make bail |
| Heroin | Late-night association with rich Brits and European jet trash | Act very hip, also nod and drool | You're too hip to say it, also too busy nodding and drooling | Your mother's heart | If there is a next day, say, "I only snort it on weekends." |

# HEROIN

Heroin and the other "downs," natural and synthetic, are not polite. These drugs effectively eliminate the painful aspect of existence, which, nowadays, is almost all of it. Pain, such as a pain in the ass, is the thing that commonly alerts us to the presence of other people. Interaction with others is what manners are all about. Don't take "downs." Try to be "down on life" instead.

# MARIJUANA

Marijuana, on the other hand, makes you sensitive. Courtesy has a great deal to do with being sensitive. Unfortunately marijuana makes you the kind of sensitive where you insist on everyone listening to all your depressing old Paul Simon tapes, and that's not very courteous.

# XTC

The drug XTC had a brief vogue in the 80s but quickly went out of fashion because it made you love everybody. Loving even one 80s person was repulsive enough; loving more than one was actually medically dangerous.

# CRACK

It's very rude to try crack a few times and not get addicted. This could throw any number of hysterical politicians and overwrought public health experts out of work.

# PRESCRIPTION DRUGS

Some drugs are considered bad form because of the image projected to the world when you take them. Valium, for instance, tells everyone you don't have a connection for good drugs like Quaaludes and have to resort to the rather pathetic expedient of getting drugs from your own doctor.

Sleeping pills send the same message. Although a whole great big fistful of sleeping pills can be a polite way to get rid of someone you can't stand—yourself, for instance.

# THE HALLUCINOGENS

The hallucinogenic drugs such as psilocybin, mescaline, and peyote are not rude *per se*. But it can be difficult to observe all the niceties of etiquette when you're being chased down the street by a nine-headed cactus demon. The mind-altering drugs are more impractical than impolite. They make you see things which aren't there, and it's a general rule of life that the things which *are* there are plenty bother enough.

# COCAINE

Cocaine is, *au fond*, the only truly polite drug. This is because cocaine makes us so intelligent, witty, charming, alert, well dressed, good looking, and sexually attractive. True, there are exceptions. Cocaine doesn't always do this to *you*. But cocaine always does this to the author.

## *The Fine Points of Cocaine Etiquette*

The most important thing to understand about cocaine etiquette is that cocaine is bad for the health. And this is why it's never bad manners to go off alone and fire some "nose Nikes" and not share them with anyone else. To risk your own health while protecting the well-being of others is the only honorable thing to do. For the same reason, when offered someone else's cocaine, you should Electrolux as much as possible for their sake. They will be less inclined to destroy their mucous membranes, become psychotic, suffer heart palpitations, or die from an overdose if there isn't any left to take.

## *Three Common Cocaine Etiquette Questions*

**1.**

**Q.** *How should cocaine be served?*
**A.** Nothing is more awkward than taking out a vial of "granulated money" in a bar or restaurant and having everyone you know expect to get some. If you try to pass the "powdered

pole-vault" to some people and not to others, you may get slugged. And that's rude. Instead, excuse yourself inconspicuously, saying something like "Well, I sure have to go to the bathroom and so do Robert and Susan and Alice, but Jim and Fred and Bob don't have to go."

**2.**

**Q.** *What should be served with cocaine?*

**A.** Most people enjoy a couple thousand cigarettes with their "face Drano." Others mix "indoor Aspen lift lines" with multiple sedatives to achieve that marvelous feeling so similar to not having taken drugs at all. But everyone, whether he wants to or not, should drink plenty of whiskey or gin. If you smell strongly of alcohol, people may think you are drunk instead of stupid.

**3.**

**Q.** *Who pays?*

**A.** There's considerable debate about this. Some say the guest should pay for cocaine as a way of saying thank you to the host. Others say the host should pay for cocaine as part of the entertainment. Most people, however, say society at large should pay for cocaine by having to watch maniacally self-indulgent stand-up comedy routines, pathetically disconnected pop music performances, and dreadful late-night anti-drug commercials on television.

# 9

## *Conversation*

*If you were to make little fishes talk,*
*they would talk like whales.*

—Oliver Goldsmith

*W*hy talk at all? How clever
and original to be silent. No one does that. But talk accomplishes many things which silence cannot.

Talk gives form and substance to vaporous emotions, room and air to hidden anxieties. It exalts the ego, perfects the self-image, and puts your mark upon the environment. When you go around the room at a party, speaking to each person in turn, you're like a cat pissing in every corner of a new apartment.

In the present philosophical haze, talk is used as a sort of foghorn for the ship of the mind. It announces your ever-shifting position on things in the hope that you will escape having your hull punctured by such metaphysical icebergs as religious fundamentalism, channeling, or support for the Sandinista government in Nicaragua. The fact that foghorns are useless for avoiding icebergs only improves the metaphor.

Talking is helpful to those with severe problems. There is a belief current that if you have a severe problem and you talk about it, this makes everything all right. If you climb on top of a building and shoot a lot of people with a high-powered rifle, you have a severe problem. If you refuse to talk about this problem, if you claim it was your brother or someone who looked like you who shot the people and you were really at the movies when this happened or maybe you were home watching TV because you don't remember for sure, your problem will only get worse. You'll be convicted of murder. But if you proudly talk about all the people you shot and how they wiggled like shiners on a fishhook and how you laughed when they died, your problem will get better. You'll be acquitted by reason of insanity. And this makes everything all right.

Of course, being insane does not make it all right to climb on top of a building and shoot a lot of people with a high-powered rifle. But this isn't a book about truth. This is a book about courtesy. It's always courteous to make people feel comfortable. If it makes you more comfortable to be a crazy person than to be a convicted murderer, then everything is all right as far as etiquette is concerned.

Talking also helps fill certain voids in existence. In a world in which we are constantly assaulted by stimuli—broadcast media, piped-in music, bright lights, bold graphics, exotic

69

scents; indeed, sounds, sights, and smells of every kind—there are still moments of quiet, repose, and calm. You can get rid of them by talking.

One thing talk can't accomplish, however, is communication. This is because everybody's talking too much to pay attention to what anyone else is saying. Real communication should be done through lawyers or by buying thirty-second spots on network television.

## HOW TO TALK

Actually people do pay attention every now and then if what's being said is intensely personal. Therefore people will always listen to flattery and gossip.

## *The Charm of Flattery*

The beauty of flattery is that it's so easy. Say anything favorable that pops into your head. Flattery is like money. It does not need to have any intrinsic worth, and neither its source nor the intended object of its use deprives it of any charm in people's eyes.

You cannot go too far with flattery, if you want to be polite. Tell people they're brilliant, beautiful, important, accomplished, and good. This is known as lying. It's very old-fashioned but still practiced by those who are smart enough to know whether they're telling the truth or not.

A much more modern approach than lying, and one that

requires less thought and energy, is to develop a lack of personal sense of judgment so thoroughgoing that you really *believe* the people you're talking to are brilliant, beautiful, important, accomplished, and good. This state can be achieved by paying no attention to anyone or anything while going fifteen or twenty years without shutting up.

## *Gossip*

Gossip is what you say about the objects of flattery when they aren't present. Gossip is very similar to flattery in that sense and judgment should play no part in its formulation. But gossip can be more solidly grounded in fact than flattery is, especially vicious gossip. Given the way most people behave these days, this should present no problem.

Never gossip about people you don't know. This deprives simple artisans like Liz Smith of work. The best subject of gossip is someone you and your audience love dearly. The enjoyment of gossip is thus doubled: To the delight of disapprobation is added the additional delight of pity.

Make sure your audience loves not only the person you're telling something nasty about, but also the kind of nastiness about which you're telling. That is, if you're speaking to thieves, gossip about someone stealing. The thieves will have an intimate understanding of the subject and in addition will be flattered that you think they're honest: if you didn't, you wouldn't be talking about stealing in front of them.

A better topic for gossip than stealing, however, is sex. This is because most sex acts take place in private and are easy to deny. Nothing indicts like a denial.

Other excellent subjects for gossip are secret drunkenness and secret drug addiction. But you can also gossip about drinking and drug-taking that are done in public and freely admitted to. If a person has no shame about his behavior, it's really your duty to supply some. Manners are supposed to increase pleasure, and half the pleasure of acting up is in the feeling of having done something forbidden and shameful.

It would be wrong, however, to think that all gossip is negative. You can also gossip about a friend's tremendous success—for instance, the fabulous movie-directing job he just got by stealing an idea from someone else and committing a perverted sex act with the producer.

Whatever your piece of gossip is, be sure to tell your audience not to say you said it. This will remind them to say you did. It's an old trick and a sneaky one, but you don't want all the gruesome stories it took you so long to dig up being circulated without attribution.

## TALKING ABOUT IMPORTANT SUBJECTS

There's more to conversation than gossip and flattery. If you're like most people, in fact, you would prefer *not* to indulge in gossip and flattery. You would prefer to talk about yourself. The problem is getting listeners. One way to do this is to disclose all your filthy habits, immoral actions, disgusting thoughts, and perverse longings. The confessional tendency in modern society is reputed by psychiatrists to be the result of a guilt neurosis concerning excess personal liberty and the breakdown of traditional values and so on. This is not true. It's just that the only way we can get anyone to listen to us when we talk about ourselves is by turning that talk into gossip of the most horrid kind possible.

Another way to get people to listen to you is by keeping them involved in the conversation. Intersperse your comments about yourself with questions about them. Tell them how successful and clever you are, and then ask them who they sleep with and how much money they make. People so love attention that they may even tell you. This brings us to a more drastic method of getting an audience: be one. Listen patiently while other people tell you about themselves. Maybe they'll return the favor. This is risky, however. By the time they get done talking about themselves and are ready to reciprocate, you may be dead from old age. Another danger is that if you listen long enough you may start attending to what's being said. You may start thinking about other people, even sympathizing with them. You may develop a true empathy for others, and this will turn you into such a human oddity that you will become a social outcast.

## REFINING YOUR CONVERSATIONAL ABILITIES

### *Strong Language*

Flattery, gossip, and self-advertisement constitute the greater part of modern conversation. Most of the rest is made up of obscene, prejudicial, or extremely blunt language. Such

## HOW TO TALK YOUNG

It's possible to take years off your mental age by speaking in a young, with-it way. This is easily done. People under the age of twenty-five are able to communicate almost entirely by means of the following ten words and phrases and a few proper nouns:

1. oh, man
2. hey, cool
3. really
4. like
5. give me a break
6. oh, wow
7. yeah
8. huh
9. you know
10. no shit

*EXAMPLE:*

Below is the "balcony scene" from Shakespeare's *Romeo and Juliet* translated into youthful contemporary speech:

*(Enter ROMEO)*

ROMEO: Oh, man . . .
(*JULIET appears above at a window*)
ROMEO: Hey, cool.
JULIET: Oh, man . . .
ROMEO: *(Aside)* Really.
JULIET: Romeo, Romeo, like give me a break.
ROMEO: Oh, wow!

> JULIET: **Romeo?**
> ROMEO: **Yeah.**
> JULIET: **Huh?**
> ROMEO: **Like, Juliet, hey, cool, you know?**
> JULIET: **Really?**
> ROMEO: **No shit.**
>
> *(NURSE calls within)*
>
> NURSE: **Will you kids shut up? I'm trying to watch TV.**

language is popular because it is useful in gaining the attention of others.

Prejudice gives force to opinions. Compare "Federal welfare programs are aimed primarily at aiding disadvantaged minority groups" to "The government gives a free ride to niggers." Which is the more pungent expression?

Likewise, obscenity enlivens bland statements. No one is going to be interested if you say, "Many young women would like to be doctors." Say, instead, "Many young women would like to be *fucking* doctors."

Bluntness, especially when combined with obscenity or prejudice, can be very handy in arguments. If you say that the U.S. shouldn't have vetoed a UN resolution condemning Israel, and someone else says the U.S. was right to veto the resolution, the result is a social mess. In the first place, it's rude to argue politics in public. And, in the second place, what you're saying doesn't have anything to do with anyone personally, so no one cares. Use strong language to take the politics out of your argument and make it personal again by saying to whoever disagrees with your position, "Fuck you."

## *Accent*

Although people are not usually listening to what you say, they may be listening intently to how you say it, trying to figure out from your accent whether you're wealthy enough to bother with. It would be rude, a waste of their time, to let them think you aren't.

Most American regional accents are not very rich sounding. But don't try to affect the lock-jawed diction of the East Coast aristocracy. This accent is theoretically polite, but George Plimpton is practically the last person alive who has it. There's been a crash program in the Ivy League colleges and the better preparatory schools to eliminate this manner of speaking so that the sons of rich men can run for political office without reminding the voters of Margaret Dumont in old Marx Brothers movies.

Other accents are even worse. A midwestern nasal twang gives listeners the impression that you have lawn ornaments in your yard. The slurs and ellipses of California speech strike the hearer as the first three danger signals of drug abuse in teen-agers. And a New York accent sounds like somebody buggering a goose with an automobile horn.

A Texas accent is safe. Texans are all thought to have money. You can acquire a Texas accent by any of the usual means of getting brain damage.

# FAKE FRENCH IN NINE *(NEUF)* EASY LESSONS

One way to say nothing while impressing people who aren't listening is to speak Fake French. Fake French lends you all the cachet of speaking French without tedious memorization or stupid Berlitz records lying around the house. Besides, no one learns real French anymore because Americans already have a language they can't understand and don't speak well—English.

## *Lesson Un: Articles*

Use *"le"* or *"la"* in place of "the," "a," and "an" to make *anything* you say sound sophisticated.

Examples:
"Pass le coleslaw."
"Open la door."

## *Lesson Deux: Prepositions*

All English prepositions can be replaced with the French prepositions *"à"* and *"de"* which mean "at," "of," "with," "on," and anything else you want them to mean because we're not really trying to speak French, so who cares?

Example:
"I'll have le cheeseburger à la french fries."

Throw in *"chez," "sur," "dans,"* and *"voilà,"* too, if you feel like it.

Example:
"I'll have sur le cheeseburger chez dans à la french fries voilà."

## *Lesson Trois: Pronouns*

"I" is *"je"* when it's the subject of the sentence and *"moi"* when you're being silly. "You" is *"Vous."* "We" is *"nous."*

Example:
"Moi loves vous."—Fake French in its ultimate form.

## *Lesson Quatre: Nouns*

Use as many as you can recall from high school French, whether you remember the correct translation or not.

Examples:
"Soir of the living dead."
"Drinks on the maison!"
"No use crying over spilt au lait."

## *Lesson Cinq: Modifiers*

All French adjectives and adverbs mean "lots of," e.g., *"très" "plus" "beaucoup,"* et cetera. Use them everywhere.

Example:
"I've très de had too much plus to drink beaucoup."

## *Lesson Six (Say "Sees"): Verbs*

There's only one French verb of any note, *"faire,"* meaning "make," "do," "be," "become," "create," and so on and so forth. The construction "faire de _____" turns any English word into a French verb.

Examples:
"Je faire de whoopee."
"Vous faire de hell out of here."

Any English word can also be turned into a French verb by adding *"-ez vous"* to the end of it.

Examples:
"Je buyez vous le drink?"
"Mais non?"
"Screwez vous, too."

## *Lesson Sept: Negation*

"No" is said in French by forming the construction "*Ne* [verb] *pas.*"

Example:
"Ne run vous hand up moi jamb pas or je smackez vous plus dans le mouth beaucoup."
(Note garbled word order to aid in "foreign" sound.)

## *Lesson Huit: Advanced Fake French*

To give the impression of a really thoroughgoing fluency, translate all your favorite English phrases into literal French with a pocket dictionary.

Examples:
"frapper la rue"
"droit sur"
"donnez moi une fracture"
"hors de vue"
"Qu'est-ce que votre signe?"
"Pas merde"

## *Lesson Neuf: Fake French in Action*

Below is the translation of an answering machine message from Babs Muddleprep, a sophomore at Bennington, to her older sister, Puffy, in Santa Barbara. The first version is given in English. The second version is in Fake French. Notice how much more, well, *je ne sais quoi* the second version is:

*Message from Babs to Puffy, translated into English:*
"I had a long talk with mother last night. There's good news and bad news. She's not drinking as much lately, but she's still really cheesed about the mess we left in her apartment. Did I tell you about the dress I found in Bendel's? It's *so cool.* But I couldn't afford it at all so I charged it to Mummy. Now she'll be pissed to the max. Have to hit the books now—French final is tomorrow and must do well because the professor is to die over. Also, I flunked the midterm. Love you bunches. See you in Sun Valley."

*Message from Babs to Puffy in its original Fake French:*
"Je faire le beaucoup chatez avec la Mother last soir. There est le news bien and le news mal. She's ne drinking pas as beaucoup lately mais she's still plus de fromaged about le mess we left dans le apartment hers. Did I tellez vous about le chemise je trouvez at le Bendel's? C'est *très froid.* Mais je ne affordez pas it at all so je chargez à Mama. Now she'll be pissoired à la maximum. Have to frapper les libres now—examination terminal de la français is demain and must faire bon because le professor est to mort sur. Aussi, je flunked le termmidi. Je t'aime beaucoup. See vous dan le Valle du Soleil.

## *Correct Usage*

If your accent is hopelessly bad and you are unable to imitate a better one, you can undo some of the damage by being extra careful with your usage. Correct use of language always makes a good impression.

*Correct Use of Language*
"I ain't got me more than no ten nor twelve million bucks that is tied up in the danged stock market."

*Incorrect Use of Language*
"At the present, I am impecunious."

## SPECIAL SITUATIONS

## *How to Start a Conversation*

If you find yourself with strangers or people you don't know well and you want to break the ice, ask them if they'd like to screw. This is flattering, concerns them personally, and will lead to lots of interesting gossip.

## *Asking Professionals for Advice*

It used to be considered bad manners, in a social situation, to ask a doctor or a lawyer for professional advice. This was before doctors and lawyers all became involved in the business of book-writing, script-consulting, and television-talk-show appearance-making. You can now ask a doctor or a lawyer anything you want about camera angles, makeup, and what studio executive is sleeping with which agent at International Creative Management.

## How to Talk on Drugs

This can especially be a problem with the drug cocaine. But don't be worried when your mouth is moving faster than your brain:

> . . . *one of the things you're really getting into is cable TV which is going to be like the rock and roll of the nineties because everybody's going to be hard-wired into 240 channels and there's this huge market for software already which is why you've got this programming development deal together that like right now is a class at the New School but is almost sold to Home Box and is going to be an hour a day that's part news but like part entertainment too like this Rap group that you've already done three minutes on with minicam on quarter-inch but you might turn that into a documentary plus maybe a docudrama for PBS because it's this sound that's sort of hip-hop but sort of western swing which is all in this interview you got with the lead singer's manager/girlfriend that you're going to publish in this magazine you're starting which will*

*be all the complete cable listings for all of New
Jersey with the public access stuff that isn't listed
anywhere plus like interviews too and . . .*

A cardinal rule of talking is that there's no reason not to
carry on a cheerful and engaging conversation just because
you're alone in the room.

# Section II

## MEN, WOMEN, AND OTHER PEOPLE

*Oh, life is a glorious cycle of song,*
*A medley of extemporania;*
*And love is a thing that can never go wrong;*
*And I am Marie of Roumania.*

—Dorothy Parker

# 10

# *Advice for Modern Women*

> *There is a tide in the affairs of women,*
> *Which, when taken at the flood, leads—God*
> *knows where.*
>
> —Lord Byron

*T*he social role of women has undergone a radical change in recent years. This is the result of feminism, and feminism is the result of a few ignorant and literal-minded women letting the cat out of the bag about which is the superior sex.

Once women made it public that they could do things better than men, they were, of course, forced to do them. Now women have to be elected to political office, get jobs as presidents of major corporations, and so on, instead of ruling the earth by batting their eyelashes the way they used to. If the mothers of Kate Millett and Susan B. Anthony had only taken more time to explain things to their daughters, it would have saved a lot of bother for more able and intelligent women like Margaret Thatcher.

## FORCING MEN TO SURRENDER

Open competition between the sexes presents considerable dangers to our society. Outnumbered and possessed of inferior capabilities, men are on the defensive. This may turn them desperate and vicious. It will be in everyone's best interests if women get men to surrender as quickly as possible.

Women can weaken the opposition by encouraging men to get in touch with their emotions. One of the few advantages men ever had over women was their emotional detachment. Think how valuable this would be to someone like Mother Teresa, who is in such constant danger of being overcome by empathy.

In the past, most men were emotionally cold and unable to show affection. Many of our fathers could come home from work to a nagging and slovenly wife and a house full of screaming brats and show no affection at all. Of course, this has changed. For one thing our parents are divorced. But, also, modern men are already much more in touch with their emotions than they used to be. They can cry—like our fathers did when they saw the court-ordered property settlement.

Do what you can to promote this trend. Make it clear to the men in your life that, not only is crying permissible, it's required if their feelings are to be given any credibility. These days it's perfectly proper for a woman to sleep with a man before marrying him or even before knowing his last name (as long as she's certain he's not a gay drug addict). But a woman who sleeps with a man before seeing his eyes mist over with need and desire is coming very close to impropriety.

Crying on demand may be too much for some men. If so, remind them that they are also expected to get erections on demand. That can make any man cry.

## VICHY GUYS

It is important, however, for women to resist the temptation to demand unconditional surrender from the male sex. Men might get cranky in defeat like Milton's Satan. They might decide that it's better to rule in the duck blinds and bowling alleys than to serve in the House of Representatives, for example. And professional bowlers are very poor alimony risks. On the other hand, Satan probably wouldn't have talked so big if God had been his wife. He would have been too busy getting brimstone out of there and installing air conditioning. Still, it's best to let men keep some vestige of their dignity, the way the Germans let the French keep Marshal Pétain.

When you go on a date with a man, it's perfectly acceptable to make it clear to him that you are harder-working, more successful, and better paid than he is. But you should also realize that he needs to retain a measure of self-respect.

Which is why, no matter how much you're making, you should let him pay for everything.

Women can also reassure men about their social position by adhering to traditional forms of address. An unmarried man is called "Mister," and a married man is called in a loud shrill voice five or six times a day on the telephone at work.

Men like to think of themselves as silent and strong. This is why women in the traditional marital role were always telling their husbands to shut up and rearrange the furniture. Modern women can achieve similar results by silencing their male subordinates at board meetings, then making decisions that result in corporate reorganization under Chapter 11 of the bankruptcy laws.

## WOMAN'S DUTY TO PRESERVE MANKIND

Besides the selfish reasons for sparing men, there is another consideration. Men are part of the earth's natural heritage. It would be a shame for the children of the future to grow up without knowing what a man looks like, never witnessing the impressive bulk of an unshaved male lying on the couch in an undershirt and boxer shorts, or seeing men only in zoos. Also, the biology of life on earth is complex. No one knows the exact role of men in the planet's biosphere. Their extinction may result in some unforeseen ecological disaster.

# 11

## Advice for Modern Men

*Here's to woman! Would that we could fall into
her arms without falling into her hands.*

—Ambrose Bierce

*S*ociety is now influenced,
shaped, and even to a large extent controlled by women. This
is a far cry from the world of our childhood, when society was
controlled by . . . Well, as the author recalls, society was
controlled by Mom. Christmas dinner for all the relatives,
square dancing, the PTA, split-level ranch houses with two
and a half baths—surely no man thought these up. Feminism
seems to be a case of women having won a leg-wrestling match
with their own other leg.

There is only one thing for men to do in response to this confusing situation, which is the same thing men have always done, which is anything women want.

## WHAT DO WOMEN WANT?

But what *do* women want? Perhaps we can shed some light on the question by examining feminist objections to traditional female social roles. Feminists believe "unliberated" women are not in control of their own lives, that they are not given adequate opportunities to realize their own potential. They feel women are overburdened with domestic responsibilities, underpaid for professional work, and exploited in every way. Of course, the average man can make the same complaints. But the cases are not comparable. Those conditions make the average man want a drink. They make the average woman want a law degree, a convertible, children, a Rolex watch, a seat on the stock exchange, two Valium, a lovely home, the lead role in a movie biography of Lotte Lenya, a pretty bracelet, the Nobel Prize, and a husband.

# FOUR RULES FOR MODERN MEN
# TRYING TO GIVE WOMEN WHAT
# THEY WANT

## 1. *Be a Husband to All Women*

No matter how liberated she is, every woman still wants a husband. No one knows why, but it's true. Even Jane Fonda has a husband. Of a sort.

Being a husband to all women is, biologically, a daunting proposition. Locker-room claims to the contrary, most of us find it's all we can do to service just one woman, let alone the whole sex. However, it is the privately held opinion of most women that their spouses are not much good for this anyway. There are other more characteristic and less physically taxing ways of acting the husband.

Even if you live alone, you should put your feet up on the furniture, smoke stinky cigars, and never take the garbage out. Identify with the role. Try to be a husband at all times. Refer to any woman within earshot as "the old lady," ask every woman you meet, "When's dinner?" and go right up to women you've never seen before in your life and tell them they've put on weight.

## 2. *Provide Orgasms*

Another of women's grievances is that male sexual techniques do not result in satisfactory female climaxes. (Personally the author is sure this is true. He did once get a woman to yell, "Oh, God! Oh, God!," but it turned out his golden retriever had bitten her on the foot.) Men must therefore be certain to provide orgasms to any females with whom they are allowed intimate contact.

The author wishes he could be more specific, but he cannot. Although he is in favor of feminism, he is still only a man and, frankly, does not know anything about where female orgasms come from. However, women seem to get a lot of what they like at cute little shops with names like "Things 'n Stuff." Maybe, next time you're at the mall, you should check it out.

## 3. Be a He-Man

He-men used to do things like fly jet fighter planes and climb Mt. Everest. They did these things to impress timorous and admiring women. Once women stopped being timorous and admiring, it was the secret hope of all us he-men that we could stop flying jet fighter planes and climbing Mt. Everest and spend the rest of our lives in a cozy restaurant with nothing more dangerous than a bad oyster for miles in any direction. Unfortunately we just look too cute in our flight suits and parkas for women to let us stop. This is why Margaret Thatcher had to invade the Falklands.

## 4. Be Helpful

Men have always been expected to be helpful to women. The same is true now but the mode of helpfulness has changed with changing sex roles. One example will suffice. In the past a man was expected to give his seat on a bus to a woman. Today it would be much more courteous for that man to give her his job.

# THE FUTURE OF THE MALE SEX

Having acquiesced to feminism, most men are adjusting to present realities. There have been no mass suicides among professional ice hockey teams or other all-male groups, and so far very few of us have been rounded up and placed in camps other than the usual fishing ones. But what does the future hold? What part will men play in the society of tomorrow? Well, women have taken our jobs and homosexuals are wearing the parkas and flight suits, and that probably means we'll be sitting around the house in our underwear watching NFL football.

Yet there's still a place in the world for men. Women want to be a lot of things traditionally considered masculine: doctors, rock stars, body builders, presidents of the United States. But there are plenty of masculine things women have, so far, shown no desire to be: pipe smokers, first-rate spincasters, wise old drunks, quiet. And there is one thing women can never take away from men. We die sooner.

# 12

# Modern Dating: Its Causes and Cures

*"Were it not for imagination, Sir, a man would be as happy in the arms of a chambermaid as of a Duchess."*

—Samuel Johnson

Dating is a social engagement with the threat of sex at its conclusion. Most dating results from lingering guilt about masturbation. Of course, no one feels religious or ethical guilt about masturbation anymore. But people do feel guilty for not being more successful. They believe if they were more successful they would have someone to handle their genitals for them and would not have to do it themselves.

Sophisticated people masturbate without compunction. They do it for reasons of health, privacy, thrift, and because of the remarkable perfection of invisible sexual partners. But, more important, they masturbate for philosophical reasons. It is an ethos of modern life that before you are able to love others you must first love yourself. And what's love without sex?

But people who are as fond of impressing others as they are of being impressed with themselves still feel compelled to have sexual "relationships." Naturally, if had at all, these relationships should be had according to the forms and usages of modern society.

## WHO SHOULD *NOT* DATE?

Polite dating is generally accepted in society, but there are some people who should refrain from doing it publicly.

• People who have just received a clean bill of health on an AIDS antibody test (because half the fun of modern dating is contained in the spectacle of two slight acquaintances trying to figure out polite ways to ask each other whether they perform anal sex with hemophiliac bisexual central African drug addicts).

• Recent widows or widowers should not take a date to the funeral.

• It's impolite for old people to date because the rest of us are disgusted at the thought of them in bed together.

• And people who have just been married are really not supposed to go out with anyone except their new mate for a few weeks at least. But, although it's rude for a bride to cheat on her husband, it would be equally rude to make her feel bad about it. Remember the famous example of the hostess whose guest mistakenly drank from the finger bowl. The hostess picked up a finger bowl and drank also. Be the same way. If your new wife is having sex with someone else, make her as comfortable as you can by having sex with that person, too.

## MEETING PEOPLE

The first consideration in dating is whom to date. "Pick-ups"—social engagements with total strangers, often initiated in bars—have gone completely out of style. Partly this is a result of AIDS, although it's a well-known fact that extra-attractive strangers (especially cute girls) never have this disease. Another, more important reason for the demise of the "pick-up" is that there are only five types of people, and— what with the exhausting vogue for meeting people in the 60s, 70s and early 80s—we've met them all.

The five types of people are:
• People whom you like more than they like you
• People who like you more than you like them
• Rich fools
• Poor fools
• People just like your parents

None of these is the type of person you're looking for.

The fashionable person to date nowadays is someone you've

known for years and somehow neglected to sleep with during the promiscuity hysteria. You'll have a lot in common with this person. One thing you'll have in common is trying to figure out if maybe you *did* sleep together and both forgot it. Then you can talk about all the people you've both slept with and whether any of them are losing a lot of weight or are dead. And when you've exhausted those two subjects, you can screw. (But never on the first date. Another well-known fact about AIDS is that it's only transmitted on first dates. You cannot get AIDS from sex you had to wait for.)

## MAKING A DATE

Dates used to be made days or even weeks in advance. Now dates tend to be made the day after. That is, you get a phone call from someone who says, "If anyone asks, I was out to dinner with you last night, okay?"

Some dates are still made in advance, of course. But it is no longer necessarily the man who does the asking. It is now considered proper for a woman to ask a man out on a date. It is not, however, considered proper for the man to refuse because he has to wash his hair. Not unless his blow dryer really is broken.

Dates are still canceled the same way they always have been, which is at the last possible moment. But it happens more often than it used to. Our society has become increasingly affluent. Therefore the probability of someone better than you coming along has improved.

## DATING BEHAVIOR

When a modern couple are out on a date, the key to behavior is equality. If you are a man taking a woman out, you should not cut up her food for her, tie her shoes, put her on your shoulders to see a parade, or perform any of the other services you would provide to a child or a trained chimpanzee. You may, though, hold a door open, light a cigarette, or assist a woman with her coat. In other words, you may extend various courtesies to a woman but only those courtesies you would extend to another man. Whether you should fondle her knee or run your hand up under her skirt is another question. Health concerns being what they are these days, the author really does not know what you would do with a male friend in a skirt under similar circumstances.

For reasons discussed in Chapter 10, men generally pay for all expenses on a date. (Exceptions are made if the woman is uncommonly rich or ugly.) Either sex, however, may bring a little gift, its value to be determined by the bizarreness of the sexual request to be made later in the relationship. Telling the difference between accepting these gifts and performing an act of prostitution is not a problem, as there is no difference.

## WHERE TO GO ON A DATE

Sex without any social relationship preceding it is tantamount to treating people like objects. People shouldn't be treated like objects. They aren't that valuable. So you have to go someplace before you screw. And that place is usually dinner.

Having dinner before sex gives you a chance to reconsider and masturbate after all. A lot of people are better imagined in your bed than found there in the morning.

## WHEN SHOULD A MAN GET AN ERECTION?

Whenever it becomes clear that a date is moving to its natural conclusion, it is then polite for a man to begin having an erection. There is no better compliment that a man can pay. To be courteous, however, a man refrains from getting an erection during kissing until the kisses have passed from the closed-mouthed "buss on the lips" to the open-mouthed "French style." A man gets a slight or salutary erection when he strokes the breasts or buttocks of his date. He should get a full erection whenever his date purposely touches his genitals. If there is a dance floor at the restaurant, a well-bred man gets an erection during close dancing but not during fast or disco dancing when he and his partner are separated and an erection would stick out and spoil the lines of his suit. Erections are perfectly proper when seated at the table, but a man should lose his immediately when he gets up to go to the bathroom. Otherwise it will look as though he has someone waiting in there. An erection in the car or taxicab after dinner is considered very good manners. And a polite man always gets an erection during sex.

## DATING PITFALLS

The one serious dating pitfall is the possibility that the person you date may contract an infatuation for you. Infatuation is much more dangerous than love or marriage. Modern marriages are happy, casual affairs, easily entered into and easily gotten out of. Modern love of one person for another is so rare that it hardly presents a problem. But now that love and marriage are no longer serious emotional concerns, infatuation is forced to bear the freight of all the human psyche's pathetic needs, drives, tensions, and energies. As a result, we have been turned into an entire society of fourteen-year-olds with crushes on our gym teacher. But, with the physical and financial freedoms of adulthood at our command, we are able to harass that gym teacher much more effectively than we could in junior high.

If you fear that your date is becoming infatuated with you, what you should do is fart, as loudly as you can, right in front of her (or him). This may seem a coarse thing to do, but it is almost impossible for someone to retain an idealized, dreamy conception of you when you've just blown the slipcovers off the furniture and killed all the pets.

# 13

# More Sex: If You Must

*Neither shalt thou lie with any beast to defile*
*thyself therewith: neither shall any woman*
*stand before a beast to lie down thereto: it is*
*confusion.*

—Leviticus 18:23

$\mathcal{S}$exual variations used to be
considered impolite for fear that servants might walk in
during them. It was thought that if the lower classes discovered the more exotic forms of sexual coupling, nothing would
ever get done around the house. Which is exactly what has
happened. Nothing gets done around the house or anywhere
else these days because the lower classes are all out dressing
up in garter belts and watching mud-wrestling matches.

Very civilized people still consider sexual variations to be rude. Normal intercourse and customary caresses should be enough if you are really in love with your sexual partner. But, since no one is (and since promiscuity is currently suicidal), sexual experimentation and even perversion have gained a sort of general social acceptance like using the same size glasses for red and white wine.

## UNUSUAL POSITIONS

There are any number of positions from which the sex act may be accomplished. Most of them are polite if your physique bears exposure at that angle, and none of them are rude with the lights off. Very modern people don't consider unusual physical positions exciting. They like unusual social positions instead. A wealthy and celebrated forty-five-year-old movie actress and a seventeen-year-old boy who parks cars at the Beverly Hills Hotel—that's considered exciting in Hollywood. On the other hand, middle-class people find this disturbing. When the actress and the car jockey start to write and direct movies together, middle-class people are disturbed at paying seven dollars to see the results.

## ORAL SEX

Oral sex is currently very trendy. It is even preferred to the regular kind. It is preferred because it's the only way most of us can get our sex partners to shut up.

A few rules of common courtesy should be observed during oral sex: Never do anything to your partner with your teeth that you wouldn't do to an expensive waterproof wristwatch. And, once you've had a good look around down there, be sure to pay your partner a compliment of some kind. Restrict quantitative compliments to men, however. "You sure have a big ass" is not considered flattery by most women.

## VANISHING SEX ACTS

A number of old-fashioned sex acts, while still correct, have fallen into disuse. This is a shame. Such practices as the dry hump had undeniable charm. It allowed a woman to investigate a man's erectile abilities without actually getting his clothes off and putting him in a position where he felt obligated to do something he could not with all the resultant dull small talk about how this happens to everyone. VISA and MasterCard have made dry humping obsolete. Easily available credit killed the notion of saving up to get something you want and thus the concept of deferred pleasure was eradicated from our society.

Without deferred pleasure there is no petting, either. Modern couples—once they've decided to couple—just strip their clothes off and go at it. In addition to credit cards, blame must also be placed on ex-President Nixon's decision to let the U.S. dollar float in relation to other Western currencies. A decade and a half of monetary instability has conditioned people to utilize their assets immediately.

Despite lobbying by the dry-cleaning industry and by safe

sex advocacy groups, the handjob is also disappearing. It's hard to understand why the handjob, with its very modern detached, impersonal character, is fading from use. Perhaps it's because jacking people off is done so much over the phone these days.

## MILD BONDAGE

The uncertain and frenetic nature of modern life has led to the increasing popularity of mild bondage. When you're tied to the bed, at least you know where you're going to be for the next few minutes. And dominant partners enjoy the sense of having control over a situation, something they never get in real life.

The dominant partner should show courtesy, however, and not abuse that position of control. It would be rude to get your sexual satisfaction by tying someone to the bed and then leaving him or her there and going out with someone more attractive.

## MORE EXTREME FORMS OF BONDAGE

More extreme forms of bondage involve homes in the suburbs, station wagons, household food budgets, and Little League coaching activities and are too alarming and repulsive to discuss in print.

## SADISM

The dominant partner in a sadistic relationship must adhere to a strict set of rules. Dominants must, in appearance, attitude, and tone of voice, always give the impression of being in charge. They must never hurt the submissive partner more than that person wishes to be hurt. They must take care not to injure the health of the submissive partner and must take all responsibility for the actions and equipment used during sex.

In general, the dominant partner must go to a great deal of bother and expense, and dominance is a very sadistic role to force anyone into.

## MASOCHISM

Masochists are people who have pain confused with pleasure. In a society which has television confused with entertainment, Doritos confused with food, and Dan Quayle confused with a national political leader, masochists are clearly less mixed up than the rest of us.

Because they are admired for their relative good sense, masochists should be careful to mind their manners. They should be especially kind to sadists, remembering that sadists are to be pitied because they find violence only sexually rewarding instead of financially rewarding the way movie producers and owners of NFL football teams do.

## CROSS DRESSING

Modern people often feel a need to take on sexual roles other than their own. This probably stems from a not unfounded idea about our personal lives that nothing could be worse than the way things are already.

The most common type of cross dressing is practiced by homosexual men who have adopted the blue-jeans, work-shirt, and construction-boot dress of heterosexual men. This has led to some unpleasantness between gay men and straight women. The women feel that it was they, not gays, who fought the battle for sexual equality and therefore it's a woman's prerogative to wear blue jeans, work shirts, and construction boots.

Some heterosexual men occasionally don pantyhose and a bra in the privacy of the bedroom, but, in general, straight men have kept a lower profile about their urge to cross-dress. Mostly they've limited themselves to puttering around the house in bathrobes and using lots of Chap Stick when they go skiing.

The only really firm rule of taste about cross dressing is that neither sex should ever wear anything they haven't yet figured out how to go to the bathroom in.

## HOMOSEXUALITY

It is the height of fashion to think, dress, and act like a homosexual. But, suddenly, it has become very unfashionable to be one. AIDS is only partly to blame. There's also the immense fatigue everyone is feeling with equality. Blacks,

Hispanics, Asians, cripples, women, and guests on *The Oprah Winfrey Show* are all demanding to be treated as equals. Homosexuals are just one more voice of complaint in an already too querulous world. If all these people want to be equal with each other, fine. But since homosexuals are often wealthy and famous, treating them as equals is not only difficult but can actually be construed as rudeness. The whole thing is a social mess.

## WIFE SWAPPING

Wife swapping is never done in the best circles of society. Wives can rarely, if ever, be traded for anything useful like a set of golf clubs.

## SEX TOYS

There are a number of mechanical devices which increase sexual arousal, particularly in women. Chief among these is the Porsche 911 Cabriolet.

## INCEST

It is very bad form to screw your children except in your will. Incest with a brother or sister is perfectly acceptable, however, as long as it is done to enliven an otherwise bland secret diary, set of memoirs, or unauthorized biography. If it is done purely for physical pleasure, though, it looks to the world like a mere convenience and reflects poorly on the social lives of you both.

## CHILD MOLESTING

It is not good manners for an adult to insist on having sexual intercourse with a child. Just as it is not good manners for a child to insist on having social intercourse with an adult. The tone of society would be greatly improved if these two axioms were adhered to.

## RAPE

Rape is extremely rude. Rape is a complete and total violation of the privacy of an individual. Despite the fact that complete and total violation of the privacy of individuals is one of our society's most popular and fashionable pastimes, rape is still considered rude. This is because rape shows the ignorance of the rapist. If the rapist had pursued the more accepted forms of privacy invasion he would know all the intimate details of his intended victim's life. When you find that much out about most people these days, you don't even want to shake their hands, let alone chase them down the street.

# 14

# Where Babies Come from and Where They Should Go

An' one time a little girl 'ud allus laugh an'
    grin,
An' make fun of ever' one, an' all her blood-an'-
    kin;
An' wunst, when they was "company," an' ole
    folks wuz there,
She mocked 'em an' shocked 'em, an' said she
    didn't care!
An' thist as she kicked her heels, an' turn't to
    run an' hide,
They wuz two great big Black Things a-standin'
    by her side,

*An' they snatched her through the ceilin' 'fore
she knowed what she's about!
An' the Gobble-uns 'll git you
Ef you
Don't
Watch
Out!*

—James Whitcomb Riley

*H*aving children is impolite. It imposes on the peace and quiet of others and leaves you with less time for that key component of courtesy, being nice to yourself. But rude things do happen. In fact they're happening at a horrific rate because the generation that refused to grow up has finally spawned, resulting in *Baby Boom II— The Terror Continues*. Suddenly there are millions of children all over the place, all of them named Jason and Rachel.

## WHERE CHILDREN COME FROM

Children are caused by having sex. Because of the media attention paid to child-napping, artificial insemination, surrogate motherhood, *in vitro* fertilization, and illegal adoption, it can be easy to forget this. But normal sex (consult your doctor) can result in pregnancy. Astonishingly enough, this is often intentional.

## WHY HAVE CHILDREN?

Humans are the only animals that have children on purpose with the exception of guppies, who like to eat theirs. Of course, nature wants every creature to produce more living things so all of us, and not just guppies, will have something to eat. But almost no one eats babies anymore. Thus there must be reasons other than natural ones for our urge to breed.

Men have children to prove they aren't impotent, or at least that some of their friends aren't. And women have children because no modern woman should reach the age of forty-five without an excuse for failing in her career. This last reason for having children is the entire cause of the current fertilization craze.

## ABORTIONS

Very busy parents should consider this option. Aborted children are inexpensive and require less quality time. And abortions are practically worry-free since there are any number of very fervent right-to-life organizations available to worry about them for you.

## PREGNANCY

A pregnant woman is expected to act joyful and, indeed, she may be quite happy if she has bulimia and enjoys throwing up.

113

Pregnant women should be given special treatment, especially by politicians attempting to garner votes by emphasizing bogus "family values" to a generation of Americans who hated their families and everything to do with them. Pregnant women should be given free prenatal care, free day care, 10,000-day paid maternity leave, Medicare, Medicaid, and daily home visits by the Surgeon General of the United States. To combat sexism, pregnant men should be given the same things. The rest of the taxpayers can go get screwed—without getting pregnant.

## INFANT CARE

Correct infant care is vital to producing "Super Babies." Super Babies are similar to regular babies except they belong to you.

Never use commercially prepared baby food; there are rumors that it causes cancer. Feed your child the same grotesque and faddish foods that you eat: soy cakes, kelp, alcohol-free beer, twelve pounds of oat bran a day—whatever dietary foolishness is current in your house. Then force the rest of your irrational activities on the child. It doesn't matter when a kid begins to walk or talk but it's very important that he should begin to work out at the gym and communicate openly with his child psychiatrist as soon as possible.

An infant should be weaned from the breast as soon as the mother has had an opportunity to shock and discomfit her boss, mother-in-law, and husband's friends by breast-feeding the baby in public.

Weaning a child from the breast is very similar to weaning an adult from alcohol or drugs. The same techniques of substitution and psychological support may be used. Babies are not, however, generally sent to the Betty Ford Clinic or AA meetings. But this might not be a bad idea. Give it a try.

## TOILET TRAINING

Modern parents believe toilet training should be an easy and casual affair. Just let the child shit all over everything. This prepares him or her for a brilliant career as a talk show host.

## DISCIPLINE

It used to be thought that children should act like "little adults." Like many things that used to be thought, this is true. In fact, now more than ever. Today's real adults are self-involved, impulsive, inarticulate, and spend as much time as possible out playing. They can't sit still, don't like to get dressed up, and hate every kind of activity that requires self-restraint. Adults are the children of today, and therefore children have to be adults because there's only so much room in the world for kids.

One way to discipline a child is by having a tantrum. Cry, scream, or hold your breath until the child behaves. When dealing with immature behavior such as nose picking, genital fondling, or public belching, try to be discreet so your child won't make fun of you when you do it.

You can also reason with even the smallest child. Tell a baby, "When you cry in the middle of the night and have to be fed and walked and burped, it, like, you know, violates my space." This is useless but instructive. It teaches both you and the child an important lesson in the powers of logic.

Spanking can be effective at times, especially since it's much less dangerous than striking a person your own size. But usually you should try to be an easygoing parent. That way the child will be much more surprised and terrified when you hit him.

Another excellent method of discipline is to ignore a child who's acting up. This may not work very well, but it certainly is easy. What people often mistake for permissiveness in modern parents is actually firm discipline exercised by means of this technique. Ignoring a child kills two birds with one stone. When you pay no attention to your kid, you're also respecting his privacy—a good way to show love while inflicting punishment at the same time.

Do not be dismayed if your child seems to want more affection than ignoring him provides. Children like a lot of affection, but they also like a lot of candy, which goes to show that children have no idea what's good for them. Explain to the child that it would be rude, a form of lying, really, to show too much affection to somebody you aren't going to sleep with.

## IMPARTING VALUES TO THE CHILD

Naturally you want a child to be mature and respectful and keep out of your hair, but simple vanity will also dictate that you want the child to turn out exactly like you. This is best accomplished by example. Yell at the child and boss him around to show him what it's like to be self-actualized and have control over his environment.

But never make a child feel guilty. One of the most persistent problems plaguing adults in our society is guilt feelings. Make it clear to the child that feeling guilt is not mentally healthy. Let him know that if he feels guilty, he's not really guilty; he's really insane.

## THE FACTS OF LIFE

The principal fact of life is, of course, death. Even very young children need to be informed about dying. Explain the concept of death very carefully to your child. This will make threatening him with it much more effective.

As for sex, modern life has made telling a child about this much easier—in fact, unnecessary. You should, however, have a "birds and bees" talk with your child just to make sure he has sex figured out by the time he's five. He's not paying much attention to the world around him if he doesn't, and maybe you should have him checked for mental retardation.

117

## MEDICAL PROBLEMS

Hyperactivity is a medical tragedy that strikes one out of every one modern children. You should see a doctor about it. Maybe he'll give your child drugs and you can steal them.

## WHEN CHILDREN GROW UP

Always remember that grown children will turn into parents themselves. Your own parents, for instance—they are nothing but grown children and you should treat them as such. Be extra lenient, however, if they've been judged still competent to change their wills.

Because of their size, parents may be difficult to discipline properly. Most modern people try to get outside help. This outside help should be outside of town in a nursing home or, even better, in a nursing home outside the state. Anyway, it should be far enough that you have an excuse for not visiting very often.

Parents should be given only a modest and sensible allowance. And they should be encouraged to save up for things. This builds character. It also helps pay for the funeral.

# 15

## *After Marriage*

*The bonds of wedlock are so heavy that it takes
two to carry them—sometimes three.*
—Alexandre Dumas

*N*othing is so satisfying to
the relatives of a young couple, so pleasing to their friends, or
so gratifying to themselves as a beautiful divorce.

## THE DIVORCE ANNOUNCEMENT

When a couple decide to divorce, they should inform both
sets of parents before having a party and telling all their

friends. This is not only courteous but practical. Parents may be very willing to pitch in with comments, criticism, and malicious gossip of their own to help the divorce along.

## ANNOUNCING THE DIVORCE IN THE NEWSPAPERS

Divorces are commonly announced in the newspaper just before either party knows the divorce is coming. A typical announcement reads:

> . . . seen out every night in New York, heart-stop-pingly handsome financier BILKMAN BANK-STOCK . . .
> Darling Mrs. BB (FLIPPSY to friends) is skiing in Gstaad . . .

A photograph usually accompanies the announcement, showing Mr. Bankstock with a sixteen-year-old Ford model.

## WHEN TO DIVORCE

There is no preferred season for divorce. It can take place at any time. But the custom of a long marriage is falling out of fashion.

A brief predivorce period is favored because it's best for final separation to take place before the romance is gone from a marriage. Otherwise the couple are likely to have no regrets. (Having no regrets is a common, even popular, modern condition. It is nevertheless to be avoided. Having no regrets is what robs modern alcoholism of poignancy. It has also ruined modern verse.)

## ASKING "CONSENT"

It is a very charming tradition for the man to go to his wife and "ask for her consent" to a divorce, even if she has been consorting with zoo chimps and the whole U.S. Navy.

In reality, of course, the man makes up his own mind first and only then asks permission from the people who matter. If his lawyer and accountant say no, that he can't afford it, continuing with the divorce is still acceptable. Shooting the wife is not—unless what's shot is a photograph of her with the monkey.

The wife may also propose a divorce to her husband, especially if she can prove he was involved with the same midshipmen as she.

Either way, the divorce should be conducted in a polite manner, which is to say there should be plenty of screaming, yelling, threats, and accusations. It would be exceedingly impolite to deprive friends and relatives of the unique pleasures attendant upon a messy divorce.

## PARTIES

Parties for the husband who's getting a divorce are given by his friends. Parties for the wife are given by her friends. At her parties, the wife first officially wears the pained expression of long-suffering decency. That expression is to be worn throughout the divorce proceedings.

When you have been a mutual friend of the married couple and cannot decide where your allegiance lies, you should always side with the richer person. Given the mercenary nature of modern divorce lawyers, the richer person will, in the end, be the one more wronged.

## WHEN A DIVORCE DOES
## NOT WORK OUT

When two people are in love, nothing gives greater perfection to their happiness than the knowledge that one or the other is getting rid of a spouse. But if things are not going well with the divorce, it is absurd, in this day and age of no commitments, to feel any untoward commitment to separation.

Some people are just not meant to be divorced. Unhappy as it may make you in the short term, staying married may have long-term benefits. You can elicit much more sympathy from friends over a bad marriage than you ever can from a good divorce.

## GIFTS

It is a nice touch for a newly divorced man's friends to get together and make him a present of some things he will need to set up a new household. Useful items include liquor, interesting phone numbers, more liquor, and, if the man is young or wants to pretend he is, drugs.

An appropriate gift to the ex-wife from the husband's friends is to give her a tumble or at least try **to**. When a woman is no longer in her first youth or has lost her figure, her own friends may want to get her something more practical. (The plug-in electric vibrators are much superior to the battery-operated kind.)

## CHILDREN

Naturally, children must be considered in a divorce—considered valuable pawns in the nasty legal and financial contest that is about to ensue. Also, if you have ignored a child in the past, a nice way to show him attention now is to launch a massive custody fight or even snatch the kid so that he can get the thrill of seeing his name and photograph on a milk carton or supermarket shopping bag.

## WHAT TO CALL FORMER IN-LAWS, ET CETERA

One difficult problem of divorce is knowing what to call an ex-mother-in-law, a former uncle by marriage, and other relatives of a discarded spouse. Most people call them "shitheels," "four-flushers," or "dirt."

New husbands or wives of former spouses may be called similar names or they may be called on the phone and told a thing or two they didn't know before. Thus one divorce begets another, and the wonderful atmosphere of romance which used to exist only for the young and single is made to pervade our entire social fabric, and civilization is improved.

# Section III

## FORMAL ETIQUETTE

*For the hoary and social curse*
*Gets hoarier and hoarier,*
*And it stinks a trifle worse*
*Than in the days of Queen Victoria,*
*When they married and gave in marriage,*
*They danced at the County Ball,*
*And some of them kept a carriage.*
*And the flood destroyed them all.*

—Hilaire Belloc

# 16

## The Recrudescence of Formal Ceremony

*"I et for two hours and din't recognize a thing I et except an olive."*
—Tom Mix (telling of a testimonial dinner given in his honor at the Hotel Astor)

For most of the twentieth century we Americans have been an informal bunch who preferred to ignore conventional social rites, dispense with pomp and circumstance, and set out high-ball glasses right on the George II sideboard without using coasters. Elaborate ceremonies with complex rituals, formalities, and taboos are the hallmarks of civilization, and we don't have one, so what the heck.

127

However, due to the past decade's enormous insider-trading profits and consequent nouveau riche insecurities, the large-scale social fêtes that were a staple of entertainment for our great-grandparents have made an enormous, loathsome comeback. And nobody knows how to behave during them.

Perhaps you will be invited to a cotillion in Grosse Pointe or a tea dance in Santa Barbara or maybe you'll trifle with somebody's daughter in Savannah and he'll insist on a duel with pistols at sunrise. Of course you won't know how to behave in these situations, no one would. Just follow the lead of your host/hostess and remember the value of nonchalance. A well-mannered person is never worried about what to do because anything can be done in a well-mannered way. And a well-mannered person is never worried about what to think because he doesn't.

Below are brief descriptions of some formal ceremonies you may encounter. Remember, no matter how elaborate and complicated such affairs may seem, you can always sneak up the back stairs, smoke a joint on the landing, and go play Nintendo "Robocop" with your butt-head host's ten-year-old son.

## THE VISIT OF EMPTY FORM

Victorian ladies used to spend a lot of time leaving calling cards at each other's houses. The lady who left the card pretended she was coming for a visit, and the lady who received the card pretended she wasn't home. Which she usually wasn't because she was out leaving a card at some other lady's house.

The purpose of this activity was to give Victorian ladies something to do all day to keep them from going lesbian while the men were off building railroads.

Calling cards were bent at the upper right-hand corner to indicate "congratulations," at the lower right-hand corner to indicate "condolence," and diagonally once, twice, and three times to make a tiny paper airplane.

The visit of empty form has now been replaced by the phone call of empty form wherein the lady who makes the call pretends she has something to say and the lady who receives the call pretends there's someone on the other line.

## TEA

Tea was one of the ten daily meals eaten during the nineteenth century when it was fashionable to be fat (the other nine were breakfast, elevenses, lunch, luncheon, tiffin, high tea, dinner, supper, and midnight snack).

Tea was properly accompanied by such food as cucumber and watercress sandwiches, which was how the Victorians managed to make even salad fattening.

All the women in the neighborhood who weren't paying enough visits of empty form used to come in to tea. The great distinction between tea and other meals was that the hostess served tea herself. This was to keep the servants out of the room while the ladies discussed whether to go lesbian or get their husbands to build something closer to home, like copper smelteries.

Tea is still popular in Washington, D.C., where any sort of useless and silly activity can always find a place.

# RECEPTIONS

A reception is a modern tea with a guest of honor who's not important enough to rate a dinner or who can't be trusted to be sober after six P.M.

An author is the usual guest of honor at a reception. Don't worry about not having read his book. It's not considered well-bred, these days, to spend time alone doing things like reading. It makes it look as though you don't have friends. Instead of praising the author's writing, tell him you "admire his work." Strictly speaking, this is true. If he didn't work, you would *not* admire his welfare payments coming out of your taxes.

The principal entertainment at a reception is watching the author try to figure out where his hostess keeps the booze.

# FORMAL LUNCHEON

A formal luncheon is a device for wrecking the middle of the day. Why anyone would take something as pleasant as lunch and mess it up with ceremony more appropriate to a church service is beyond understanding. You might as well have a funeral for your food. In fact, that would be more interesting. Get some china with a black border. And serve a beef dish by having it pulled into your dining room on a gun carriage drawn by a riderless black stallion with a couple of gravy boats turned backward in the stirrups. This should rate a photo spread in *People* magazine, which a formal luncheon never does.

## GARDEN PARTIES

Garden parties are afternoon affairs that were extremely popular in the early years of this century. They were encouraged by nationalistic European governments in order to make people so bored that they were willing to have a First World War—anything to get out of attending another garden party.

Garden parties consist of standing around in the garden. That's all. Sometimes sticky little drinks are served. The only way to get a worthwhile amount of alcohol out of these is to dunk your whole head in the punch bowl. As a matter of fact the real cause of the First World War was a German ambassador doing just that at a Royal Garden Party at Buckingham Palace. (For public consumption, however, a story was circulated about Archduke Ferdinand's assassination.)

## DANCES AND BALLS

Rich people didn't use to go to nightclubs. They used to dance in their own houses. That way they never had to go home to get more drugs. Also, rich people had very big houses in those days and couldn't think what else to do with some of the rooms.

Dances were sometimes given in the afternoon. These were called "tea dances" and were held to show the neighbors that you were so rich you didn't need a job and could do anything you wanted in the middle of the day no matter how expensive and wasteful.

More often, dances and balls were held at night. Dances

were small affairs. True balls were much larger and were always distinguished by a bright red carpet on the sidewalk outside the house. Then as now, that's what tasteful people did with bright red carpets—threw them out on the sidewalk. Balls also had two bands, so that there was continuous music and no excuse for getting caught with somebody else's wife in the orangery between numbers.

A really elaborate ball with prearranged dancing partners for each piece of music was called a "cotillion." The main activity at cotillions was the performance of "duty dances." These were dances with huge fat people vaguely related to your mother.

All dances and balls lasted until four in the morning and people were so dressed up that they had to be moved onto the dance floor by servants with block-and-tackle rigs. Rich people were very glad when nightclubs came along. They sold their big houses to funeral directors, slipped into something comfortable, and ran down to El Morocco, the Stork Club, and other such places to watch Hollywood types get into fistfights with photographers. They're still there.

## CHARITY BALLS

A charity ball is like a dance except it's tax-deductible. This is a wonderful invention. Unfortunately there are more people who want tax deductions than there are charities to give dances for. At last count the only charities left that did not have charity balls attached to them were:

• Relatives by Marriage of Victims of Epstein-Barr Syndrome

- Recovering Shopaholics
- Children Who Are Afraid of Being Kissed by Fat Girls While Playing Post Office
- The Dizziness from Standing Up Too Fast Fund

## DEBUTS

In its original form, a debut was the formal occasion upon which a young lady left the innocent pleasures of girlhood and was introduced into adult society. That was before the innocent pleasures of girlhood came to include three abortions, several long visits to thousand-dollar-a-day drug rehab clinics, and a summer vacation spent following the Grateful Dead tour. Nowadays the purpose of debuts is to show middle-aged bachelors how rich you are in hopes of tricking one of them into taking a maniac daughter off your hands.

A debutante party is basically a bar mitzvah with sex in the parking lot. The same rules of egregious display, inedible food, and ridiculous expense are enforced. Presents are not given, however. And—inasmuch as debuts are WASPy activities—presents like having a tree planted in Israel might actually be unwelcome.

The proper behavior at a debutante party is for the young lady in whose honor the party is being given to act like a bitch and for all the young men her age to get drunk and throw each other in the country-club swimming pool. There are some very definite rules about throwing people into swimming pools:

- Never throw anyone into a pool unless he is wearing something expensive that will be ruined by the water. (The whole point of throwing people in swimming pools is to recapture a sort of Kennedy administration insouciance. Kennedy administration insouciance presupposes such great wealth that things like rust-jammed Cartier wristwatches are expected to be laughed off as a good joke in the morning.)

• Never throw anyone into an empty pool unless you don't like him much.

• Never throw a waiter into the pool. This is excessively democratic and a total waste of all the drinks he was carrying on his tray.

• Never throw the debutante's mother into the pool unless you plan to have sex with her in the parking lot later.

• Never throw anyone into the pool if she's in her car. This brings back bad memories for the Kennedy family and will wreck all the insouciance for sure.

An additional difference between a bar mitzvah and a debutante party is that the hora is never danced at a debut. The bunny hop is, however. Bunny hops are not considered any fun unless they go through the country-club kitchen breaking lots of dishes and in one door and out the other of someone's BMW convertible. The purpose of the bunny hop, like the purpose of many group activities, is to do extensive damage that cannot be attributed to any one person. A more sophisticated version of the bunny hop is the conga line, where plate-glass windows may be more easily kicked out.

## COCKTAIL PARTIES

A cocktail party is what you call it when you invite everyone you know to come over to your house at six P.M., put cigarettes out on your rug, and leave at eight to go somewhere more interesting for dinner without inviting you. Cocktail parties are very much on their way out among rug-owning, hungry, snubbed people.

Another reason for the cocktail party's decreasing popularity is that modern health-conscious people do not drink as much as they used to—it interferes with their drug rehabilitation program.

But cocktail parties are still useful if you have a lot of cheap liquor and friends you want to get rid of.

Much more chic than a cocktail party is an invitation for people to "come over for drinks after dinner." This makes your guests think they're going to meet people more important than they are—people important enough to be invited to dinner itself. With social status thus assured, the wise host dines alone.

## TESTIMONIAL DINNERS

Testimonial dinners and other public banquets are versions of the formal dinner party. The difference is that a few particular fools are singled out and made to sit on the dais. The dais is a great place for honored women guests to show everyone their underpants.

Customarily there are speeches at testimonial dinners. These speeches are read from the phone book. At least the author believes this to be the case. They *sound* as though they're read from the phone book, and that's about how much attention anybody pays to them.

The important part of a testimonial dinner is the giving of

toasts. Toasts should progress gradually in the outlandishness of their praise. Early in the proceedings a simple "a credit to his county Republican organization" will do fine. Save until late in the evening such toasts as

> *Here's to Frank, a helluva pal*
> *Every gal's guy and every guy's gal*
> *He's a brick, he's a topper*
> *He can sing, he can dance*
> *And he frightens the horses*
> *When he lowers his pants.*

## CEREMONIES THAT HAVE NOT RECRUDESCED BECAUSE WE NEVER SUCCEEDED IN GETTING RID OF THEM IN THE FIRST PLACE

### Christmas

Christmas begins about the first of December with an office party and ends when you finally realize what you spent, around April fifteenth of the next year.

Christmas has replaced Lent as a period of penance. Christmas is when you punish yourself for having spent eleven months claiming to be friends with a pack of useless and nasty people you hardly know. Now you're forced to go out and buy each of them an expensive gift. In return you'll receive a dozen bottles of strawberry-flavored wine cooler and a pair of Louis Vuitton earmuffs.

There is a remarkable breakdown of taste and intelligence at Christmastime. Mature, responsible, grown men wear neckties made out of holly leaves and drink alcoholic beverages with raw egg yolks and cottage cheese in them. Otherwise reasonable adult women start hinting to their dates about emerald bracelets before they've even been French-kissed. The only thing that's even slightly interesting about Christmas is that office party. It's nice to see the people at work *admitting* that they're drunk and not getting anything done.

The worst part of Christmas is dinner with the family, when you realize how truly mutated and crippled is the gene stock from which you sprang.

It's customarily said that Christmas is done "for the kids." Considering how awful Christmas is and how little our society really likes children, this must be true.

## Thanksgiving

Thanksgiving is a sort of trial run for Christmas, especially for Christmas dinner. Thanksgiving is when that mysterious large and tasteless animal (supposed to be a bird but more closely resembling a stewed beachball) is first placed upon the table. This will be sliced apart and put on everyone's plate and then collected from the plates and put back together and served again at Christmas.

A number of other remarkable things show up in holiday dinners, such as "dressing," which is a loaf of bread that got hit by a truck full of animal innards, and pies made out of something called "mince," although if anyone has ever seen a mince in its natural state he did not live to tell about it.

Thanksgiving is so called because we are all thankful that it comes only once a year.

## New Year's

The proper behavior all through the holiday season is to be drunk. This drunkenness culminates on New Year's Eve, when you get so drunk you kiss the person you're married to. The hangover begins the next day and lasts through Super Bowl Sunday, when you lose whatever money you had left from Christmas by betting on the Toronto Blue Jays, who are not even a football team. The rest of the holiday season is spent adding up bills.

# 17

# The Horrible Wedding

*Beware of all enterprises that require new clothes.*

—Henry David Thoreau

No matter how socially important a wedding is and no matter how glamorous the ceremony and lavish the entertainment, everyone concerned should keep in mind that the purpose of marriage is to sanctify the solemn union of two souls in the eyes of God, and, therefore, the whole thing is a crock.

# THE PROPER TYPES OF INVITATIONS

If possible, invitations should be sent to every person in the world. If you don't have every person in the world's home address, you can still send invitations to every person you've ever met or heard of. That way you'll have a shot at the international record for the number of Cuisinart food processors received as wedding gifts. (The current record is held by Mr. and Mrs. David Careerstein of White Plains, New York, who received sixty-eight at their wedding in 1983.)

There are two basic forms of wedding invitations—the expensive engraved traditional form and the obnoxious cute Xeroxed form. Proper wording on the obnoxious cute Xeroxed form is:

> **Bingy & Babbo**
> **are getting married**
> **FINALLY!!!!!!!!**
> **(just going to the Justice of P. at the courthouse**
> **with Mom and Bingy's brother, so screw that**
> **part . . .)**
> **But come to the**
> **BIG PARTY**
> **Twin Pools Country Club 1400 Woodgrain Rd.**
> **7 pm till ???  June 15th  B.Y.O. Main Squeeze**

The above to be either hand-printed or cleverly composed in computer type and decorated with heart-shaped smile faces or ill-rendered drawings of Garfield the cat.

The expensive engraved traditional form of wedding invitation may prove more practical in the long run since the

140

engraving plates can be altered slightly and used for the bride's subsequent weddings.

## RESPONSE TO WEDDING INVITATIONS

It's traditional for the groom's friends to respond to a wedding invitation by getting the groom drunk and trying to convince him to run off to Tahiti before it's too late. The groom does not usually take this advice. And when the groom, after two or three years of marriage, actually does run off to Tahiti he is rarely grateful for his friends' prescience.

## WEDDING GIFTS

If you go to a wedding you are obligated to bring a gift, usually a Cuisinart food processor. A more personal gift would be to absent yourself from the ceremony if your relationship with the bride has been tangled and ugly in a sexual way. This can be a surprising present if you happen to be the groom, but it's apt to be appreciated in the long run.

The more traditional type of wedding gift is a large, ugly, expensive, and unreturnable thing made out of silver, cut glass, and mahogany and engraved with some peculiar piece of information such as the date and place of the bride's uncle's demobilization from the Army in World War II. This gift object is not considered perfect if its purpose can be ascertained. The very best sort might be a punch bowl or maybe an end table.

The most modern gifts are a home AIDS test and advice, usually about running away to Tahiti, but sometimes about the tangled and ugly sexual relationship you had with the bride.

The only gift that anyone ever wants, of course, is money. This is usually presented by the bride's family and can be given in two ways—either in a way that publicly humiliates the groom or in a way that publicly humiliates the groom later.

## RETURNING GIFTS

In case a wedding is canceled, the bride and groom should pretend there was a robbery. However, there is no excuse for canceling a wedding, since weddings are almost always canceled within a couple of years anyway. Therefore a wedding should go forward under any circumstances and *then* the bride and groom should pretend there was a robbery. Not only won't they have to give the gifts back, they'll get all the insurance money besides.

## GIFTS TO THE WEDDING PARTY

It is customary for the bride and groom to give something to the ushers, maids of honor, and other members of the wedding party. An excuse not to be in the wedding is a particularly thoughtful thing to give them.

## THE TROUSSEAU

The trousseau was traditionally made up of the bride's personal clothing and items she brought with her to the marriage to help set up house—towels, linen, glassware, silver, and so on. The modern bride brings a very different set of items to her marriage:

- 3 cats
- 1 child from a previous marriage
- 1 Conran's sofa bed with Azuma bedspread stuck in the fold-out mechanism
- 1 butcher block dinette set
- the complete works of Barbara Cartland
- 1 Cuisinart to match those received as wedding presents
- 1 7' × 12' mud-colored post-abstract impressionist painting by her first husband's male lover
- 3 framed drawings of unicorns
- 2 hairdryers (both broken)
- 258 cute refrigerator magnets
- 1 cat-hair-covered oriental rug
- 1 "art deco" bathroom mirror
- 1 Sony Walkman
- 1 5-year-old Honda Civic
- 1 box of loose tape cassettes (Hall and Oates, Air Supply, ABBA, George Michael)
- 1 lettuce dryer

- 1 half-dead ficus tree
- 1 pair of $600 Maud Frizon alligator pumps
- 23 framed photographs of the first husband
- 2 copies of *The Beverly Hills Diet*
- 1 signed M. Scott Peck paperback
- 50 Valium
- 1 mismatched set of Melmac plastic picnic dishes
- 3 antique glass paperweights
- 1 Crockpot
- 1 Jane Fonda workout tape
- 1 bill for $5,000 from her analyst

## MAKING ARRANGEMENTS
## FOR THE CEREMONY

It's important that a marriage be performed by someone with the legal power to do so; otherwise the two people are just living together and will *never* be able to get a divorce. Ministers, judges, and civil magistrates can all perform marriage ceremonies. So can the captain of a boat under certain circumstances, but not if it's an outboard. Maître d's at expensive restaurants cannot perform marriages. Neither can the bride's analyst, no matter how high his fees are. Amazing though it may seem, marriages performed by TV evangelists are recognized as legal in most states, although Home Divorce Club phone-in annulments are not.

Try to hire an old-fashioned cynical functionary who'll rattle off the service at high speed. Marriage is just the right moment for a traditional touch like that. Avoid ministers with the contemporary vice of sincerity, who might stop in the middle of the ceremony and say, "Are you two *sure* about this?"

## CHOOSING A TIME AND PLACE FOR THE WEDDING

The old joke was that the bride's father determined the time of the wedding with a shotgun. It's an interesting note on social progress that, metaphorically speaking, modern people hold the gun to their own heads. Wedding time is nowadays determined by the following factors:

• When two infatuated people receive negative AIDS antibody tests from their doctors during the same week

• When a man reaches the age at which he can no longer face one more date with a bond salesperson in shoulder pads who wear Reeboks with her Bergdorf Goodman business suit

• When a woman has stayed single long enough to prove that she doesn't need to get married to establish her identity and also long enough that all her girlfriends are married already

• When a couple have lived together for so many years that they need something new to fight about

• When a successful man needs to prove to bankers and investment capitalists that he isn't gay

• When a successful woman needs someone to reassure her on weekends that she's successful during the week

• When the palimony lawyer gives a bad prognosis

In the case of a very young couple a wedding may also be set when both of them are under the temporary misapprehension that each will want to fuck the other more than twenty-five times.

As for the actual time of day that a marriage takes place, it couldn't matter less. The couple will still be just as married when the ceremony is over, even if it did take place on a mountaintop at dawn. Incidentally, all the cute and novel places to have a wedding have been used up. This is why couples have returned to traditional church weddings, holding the ceremony in a large, impressive building where nobody in either family has been since the bride's mother's christening.

## MUSIC

While it's perfectly acceptable for the bride's brother's performance art ensemble to play at the reception, when it comes to the wedding ceremony itself you may find it hard to march down the aisle to the tune of "O Superman" by Laurie Anderson. Stick with Mendelssohn and don't let the groom's sister play it on a recorder, no matter how therapeutic her drug therapist says it would be.

## PHOTOGRAPHS

Normal professional wedding photographs are of no interest at all and you might as well steal somebody else's. They all look the same and this method is cheaper.

The really interesting stuff that happens at weddings never

gets photographed—though it might be fun to try. Hire someone with a Minox to circulate unobtrusively among the guests. See how many of the following shots he can get:

- Bridesmaids who've lost their underwear
- Children under fifteen throwing up from champagne
- Old men who get erections dancing with the bride
- Groom's father taking a leak in the potted plant
- Examples of how rental tuxedos fit in the seat
- Fight over whether groom will take golf clubs on honeymoon
  Et cetera.

## THE WEDDING ATTENDANTS

Ushers and bridesmaids are part of an important wedding tradition. The tradition is for the ushers to get completely drunk, wreck a couple of hotel rooms, and screw all the bridesmaids, and for the bridesmaids to get hysterical and, often, pregnant. If the friends of the bride and groom aren't brain damaged enough to act the part they should try picking ushers and bridesmaids from each other's families. If even these people are too well behaved, most cities have shelters for the homeless where winos and bag ladies can be enlisted.

Flower girls, ring bearers, junior bridesmaids, and the like are relatives of the bride and groom who are too young to serve any purpose in the ceremony but too hyperactive and unruly to sit in the audience.

The bride usually has one friend who wanted to marry the groom herself. This girl should be maid of honor so the bride can rub it in.

The best man should be that friend of the groom's with the best drugs, fewest ethics, and most ability to cause trouble behind the bar by giving bourbon and cocaine to the ushers, XTC and Kahlúa to the bridesmaids, saltpeter martinis to the groom, a Mickey Finn to the bride's mother, and vodka-laced Shirley Temples to the six-year-old flower girl. The best man's principal responsibility, however, is to talk the groom into running away to Tahiti at the last minute after all.

## SHOWERS

The old-fashioned shower was given by a bride's friends to provide her with practical items for housekeeping. But now that brides are all career women instead of housekeepers, they've lost any sense of the practical and go to the office every day and waste time and money just like men. Therefore the shower needs to be brought up to date. Perhaps a modern bride should be given a "career shower" to which all her friends would bring fascinating job offers from major corporations in cities thousands of miles away from her new husband. Another idea would be an "adultery shower" where the guests each bring someone the bride might like to have an affair with at work.

## BACHELOR PARTIES

Bachelor parties are a last fling before marriage. A young lady with very few clothes is usually engaged for entertainment purposes. The groom, the best man, and the ushers will all, years later, claim to have had sex with her, although actually they just grabbed her behind while she danced the "bugaloo" with her brassiere off.

The only really good kind of bachelor party is the kind that takes place in Tahiti after the groom has decided to stay a bachelor.

## WEDDING REHEARSAL DINNER

These days the honeymoon is rehearsed much more often than the wedding. It's not necessary to give a dinner every time you do that. Although a snack might be nice.

## DRESS FOR THE WEDDING

To all appearances the purpose of modern weddings is to make a mockery of traditional values. Therefore the bride should wear white unless she completely overdid it at the tanning salon and you can see her scorched butt right through the dress and it looks like a huge pumpkin.

The groom should be dressed to look as silly as he'll feel when he realizes what he's got himself into.

Everyone else should wear something that looks good when sprayed with champagne.

If you're a guest and want to have a little fun, you can arrive in tennis whites with a racket and a can of balls and when the minister comes to the part where he says, "Speak now or forever hold your peace," you can stand up and object to the marriage taking place at the only time of day when there are courts free at the club.

## WEDDING RINGS

Wedding rings should not be worn through the nose, no matter what Lisa Bonet does.

## WEDDING PUBLICITY IN THE NEWSPAPERS

If the wedding doesn't get any publicity in the newspapers, the groom isn't as rich as he said he was.

## THE WEDDING CEREMONY

### The Processional

The customary order of the processional is ushers first, paired by height, bridesmaids paired by width, maid of honor, ring bearer, flower girl, bride and bride's father, and one confused usher who got there late.

The interesting thing about the processional is how the

members of the wedding behave themselves as they go down the aisle. The ushers should be manfully trying to suppress laughter over something filthy the shortest one said. The bridesmaids should be holding their stomachs in and trying not to look fat in the ridiculous bridesmaid dresses. The maid of honor should have a look of knowing irony and let her eyeballs roll toward the sky every couple of steps. The ring bearer should be pretending he's a stormtrooper and do a goose step down the aisle. The flower girl should drop the flowers and howl like a baboon. And the bride's father should push straight ahead with a fixed drunken stare as the bride counts the number of people there.

The confused usher should run out and have a drink in a nearby bar until the thing's over.

## The Recessional

The recessional is conducted in the reverse order except that the groom now pushes ahead with a fixed drunken stare while the bride's father throws up behind the altar.

It's considered bad manners to stick your foot out into the aisle and trip anyone until the recessional.

## Grouping at the Altar

Everyone will crowd around the altar in a confused knot if the rehearsal was enough fun that they're all still hung over. Wedding attendants should not be concerned about this. Weddings are not like tag. Even if you do wind up standing right in front of the minister with the bride's dad breathing gin fumes in your ear, it will still be the bride and groom who get married.

## GIVING THE BRIDE AWAY

Brides are given away because it's illegal to sell them and impossible to get anything for them in trade except an out-of-work son-in-law.

## THE SERVICE

Gone forever are the days when the bride and groom were expected to write their own ceremony based on the Chinese Red Army wedding service and the *I Ching*. But it's still nice to modify traditional wording somewhat to personalize the ceremony.

The following modification of the Episcopal service is given as an example. It's brief and practical, too (note how time and location of the reception are given in the opening address to the congregation):

> *The celebrant, facing the persons to be married, addresses the congregation and says:*
> **Dearly beloved: We have come together in the presence of God to witness and bless the joining together of this man and this woman in holy matri-**

mony and to have some drinks and a big buffet dinner at Twin Pools Country Club, 1400 Woodgrain Road, right after the ceremony. The bond and covenant of marriage was established by God in creation, and the union of husband and wife is intended by God to prevent men from sleeping until two in the afternoon on Sundays and to comfort women with a greater VISA card credit line than they can achieve when they are single. Into this holy union _____ and _____ now come to be joined. If any of you can show just cause why they should not lawfully be married, just go and play tennis, will you? And they'll give you back the food processor.

*The celebrant then says to the woman:*

_____, will you have this man to be your husband; to live together like you have been for the past three years and not get weird-acting all of a sudden just because you're married now? And will you give him a break about leaving towels on the bathroom floor?

*The woman answers:*
I will.

*The celebrant says to the man:*

_____, will you have this woman to be your wife and not yell at her when you find out that she told her mother that the two of you will spend Christmas at her house in Dayton?

*The man answers:*
Okay.

*The celebrant then addresses the congregation, saying:*
Let's get a drink.

## THE RECEPTION

Wedding receptions differ according to types of excess, the type of excess being determined by religious affiliation. There is an excess of relatives at a Catholic wedding, an excess of food at a Jewish wedding, and an excess of station wagons at a Protestant wedding so that people have to park all over the grass.

Everyone should get excessively drunk at any wedding reception, although Protestants usually run out of liquor almost immediately and the men have to go in the country-club locker room and get the Scotch bottles out of their golf bags in order to get as drunk as they properly should.

## THE RECEIVING LINE

Everyone in the wedding party is expected to stand in the receiving line except the ushers and the best man. Even the most stringent authorities on etiquette have given up trying to get the ushers and best man to behave.

As you go through the receiving line say "What a lovely wedding" to each person. The correct response will be "How nice of you to come," except for the bride, who will say, "Thank you for the Cuisinart food processor," and the groom, who will say, "Bring me a drink."

(It's considered rude to slip your dick into anybody's hand as you go down the receiving line, no matter how much you're tempted to do so.)

## TOASTS

The first toast to the bride should come from the best man, who is expected to avoid complimenting her on her skill in bed, at least in so many words. Remember that brides are not supposed to be congratulated. Congratulate the groom instead; it's probably the last occasion you'll have to do so until the divorce. Toasts should go on until the men have to go to the locker room and get the Scotch bottles out of their golf bags. Do not throw the glasses into the fireplace if it's more than forty feet away.

## FOOD

Wedding-reception food, whether served at tables or presented at a buffet, should be stuff that's easy to throw up, like spaghetti.

## THE CAKE

If the groom is a military officer, the cake is traditionally cut with his dress sword. However, if the groom is an arbitrage specialist or trader in the junk bond market, no attempt should be made to cut the cake with a subpoena.

## DANCING

Members of the wedding party are expected to perform "duty dances" with all sorts of old, boring, and physically repulsive relatives of the bride and groom. This can be more amusing than you'd expect if the bride can get her brother's band to knock it off with the Laurie Anderson and play something you can slam-dance to.

## THROWING THE BOUQUET

Just before the bride leaves to dress for the honeymoon, she is supposed to throw her bouquet to the bridesmaids. Some brides see this as old-fashioned and prefer to throw something symbolic of a modern woman's independent role in the home and workplace—a word processor, for instance.

## KISSING THE BRIDE

Kissing of the bride by male wedding guests is today considered sexist and demeaning (and a possible source of infection with sexually communicable diseases). Instead, slap her on the backside as you would a football teammate.

## SEEING THE BRIDE AND GROOM OFF ON THE HONEYMOON

Under no circumstances should pork fried rice be thrown in place of the regular kind and shoes should not be attached to the back of the groom's car if the groom is still in them.

## ELOPEMENT

Elopement is a very unsatisfying method of getting revenge on your family for their objections to your marriage. It's much more spiteful to make them pay for an immense wedding reception even if you have to marry someone they like to get them to do it.

## SECOND, THIRD, FOURTH, FIFTH, SIXTH, AND SEVENTH MARRIAGES

There is no rule of etiquette that says subsequent marriages shouldn't be as horrible as the first. Make them as elaborate, dressy, and expensive as you like. But don't expect anyone to attend past the third one, and that includes your betrothed.

# WEDDING ANNIVERSARIES

Wedding anniversaries are no longer much of an etiquette problem, since there are rarely more than two. Thus the tradition of certain types of gifts for certain anniversaries (silver for twenty-fifth, gold for fiftieth, et cetera) has been rendered obsolete. Given below, however, is a proposed new list of gift themes for all the anniversaries a modern couple is likely to have:

**First**—Drug Anniversary (Give XTC, *sinsemilla*, Retin-A.)

**Second**—Decision Not to Have Children Anniversary (Give fitness equipment or vacation accessories.)

**Third**—Woman's Career Anniversary (Give something to husband to make him feel better about making less money than his wife.)

**Fourth**—Decision to Have Children After All Anniversary (Give cash.)

**Fifth**—Divorce Anniversary (Give moral support, sympathetic ear.)

# COMMONLY ASKED QUESTIONS ABOUT WEDDING PROTOCOL

**Q.** *Is the bride's father expected to pay for all the expenses of a wedding?*

**A.** If the bride is good enough at forging his signature, he'll have to.

**Q.** *How should family members be seated at the wedding?*
**A.** On their asses.

**Q.** *Should I really go through with this?*

**Q.** *Where can I get a drink?*

# 18

# The Hip Funeral

*Squares*
*Who couldn't dig him,*
*Plant him now—*
*Out where it makes*
*No diff' no how.*

—Langston Hughes

Death, like marriage, is a social event and can be quite a chic one if the dead person is a rich parent and you inherit enough money to become fashionable. Dying yourself, however, is considered outré.

If you must die, try to be considerate about it. Don't make antismoking commercials to be shown on TV after your death.

160

Be certain your section of the "Names Project" AIDS memorial quilt isn't decorated with teddy bears or glitter. If possible, die in a manner that entertains people while also impressing them with your attributes. Choking to death during autofellatio is an example. And die young to create a livelier and more with-it funeral crowd.

## THINGS TO SAY WHEN DYING

If you're going to die in public, have something memorable ready to say:

• "Oh, my gosh! There's angels and God and Jesus and pearly gates and St. Peter and everything!" (Memorable if your family is orthodox Jewish.)

• "Goodbye, Mary. I love you. Goodbye." (Memorable if your wife's name is Sue.)

• "There's a million dollars buried in the yard right by the . . . by the . . . arrrrgh." (Definitely memorable and good if the lawn needs to be dug up and reseeded.)

• "It was me; I kidnapped the Lindbergh baby." (Memorable but no good if you're under seventy-five.)

• "Go fuck yourselves, the bunch of you." (Trite, but will definitely be remembered by everyone present.)

# IMMEDIATE STEPS UPON DEATH OTHER THAN YOUR OWN

First, make sure the deceased is actually dead. A rich parent can get very testy if you start building a subdivision on the grounds of her summer house when it turns out she's only taking a nap. Then tie up the book and movie rights. A rights deal is especially important if the deceased is young, well known, and died of drugs or other causes with hot commercial potential. Don't forget television, both broadcast and cable, and such merchandising possibilities as T-shirts and novelty items. Christina Crawford's failure to license a line of wooden coat-hangers is proverbial.

# BREAKING THE NEWS

The family members and close friends of the deceased should be informed of the death as soon as possible after you've wiped your fingerprints off the syringe and called your agent. Someone who's not in the immediate family should be appointed to make the necessary calls, someone like your agent. But try to call the deceased's mom personally. What she says could make an interesting cover blurb or lead sentence to your book.

You may want to make some of the other calls yourself, too, since announcing the death of a mutual friend is an excellent occasion for patching up old quarrels or introducing yourself to people you've always wanted to meet.

## DEATH NOTICES

The standard form of the newspaper death notice is:

> Moresnort—Elliot, on January 3rd, beloved husband of Jennifer Windbrain Moresnort and father of Paisley and Shadrack Moresnort, after a brief illness. Funeral at Le Mortuary, Little Santa Monica Blvd., Beverly Hills, at 2 P.M., Tues., January 6th. No flowers. Donations may be sent to the No Nukes for the Homeless Committee, Box 462, Mill Valley, Ca.

This is hopelessly dull and can be livened up thus:

> Moresnort—Elliot "Bonkers," on January 3rd, somewhat beloved husband of Jennifer Windbrain Moresnort, somewhat less beloved ex-husband of Annette Dimlit Moresnort, totally unbeloved ex-husband of Lee Ann VanLay Moresnort, father of Paisley and Shadrack who would much rather be called Betty and Jim Moresnort, alleged father of twins in Redondo Beach, after fourteen magnums of Cristal, half an ounce of cocaine, six Quaaludes, ten Valium, and a whole bunch of heroin. Funeral at Le Mortuary, Little Santa Monica Blvd., Beverly Hills, at 2 P.M., Tues., January 6th. No flowers. No drugs either, his parents are going to be there. Donations may be sent to the No Nukes for the Homeless Committee, Box 462, Mill Valley, Ca. Information may be given to the LAPD.

163

Where there is press coverage of a death, remember to be considerate of the deceased's family. Tell reporters, "Bonkers never *touched* drugs!" This also shows consideration for his coke connection. But also remember that good manners mean being considerate of everyone and that includes members of the press. Tell them, "Since it wasn't drugs, it must have been murder." This will give them something to write about and keep them busy tracking down false leads while you finish your book.

## DONATION OF ORGANS

The best thing to do in the way of organ donations is to donate your organ to comfort the attractive young widow.

## THE WILL

Video wills should have an MPAA rating no stronger than PG-13. "Living Wills" should be very specific about the definition of "brain dead" and not so carelessly worded that they can be enacted by greedy heirs if your foot goes to sleep.

The author advises against trying to make funny bequests. Everything novel and amusing that can be done with a last will and testament has already been used as a Movie-of-the-Week plot device. An exception might be made if you can get your will spelled out by the card section at the annual Ohio State–Michigan football game:

I LEAVE
EVERYTHING
TO MY 6 CATS

## FUNERAL ARRANGEMENTS

Funerals have lagged behind other social events in modernization. Many people write their own wedding ceremonies these days, but very few write their own funerals. It would be terrifically *au courant* to do so. A suggested form is given below:

**I'm dead now. Everybody who really loved me, take off your pants.**

Creativity has also been stifled in the matter of funeral locations. A more appropriate place for a modern funeral than a church or a mortuary would be a psychiatrist's office or the backseat of a car. Family members tend to resist such innovations, but if the deceased's mother and father really object they can kill themselves and have any kind of funeral they want.

## CLERGY

Modern people, of course, have no religion. It's very unmodern to believe in anything for more than ten minutes. Since most religions are at least five hundred years old, they are out of the question. The deceased's parents, however, tend to turn to religion for solace in the face of a death they cannot understand (having no experience with drugs and gross sexual promiscuity, they can't be expected to realize that their kid should have been dead years ago).

Anyway, a clergyman should be allowed to officiate at a funeral only on the condition that he be perfectly honest in his eulogy:

> **Elliot attended Sunday School at this church, intermittently. He stole a number of things and once cracked a choir member's skull with a collection plate he was employing as a Frisbee. Personally I hadn't seen him for eighteen years, although I read about him frequently in the newspapers. Believe me, I was appalled. I understand he was good to his parents insofar as he did not publicly announce their identities and place of residence and thus drag their names through the mud with his own. It would be un-Christian for me to say that I'm glad young Elliot is dead. I won't go that far. But it is beyond me what purpose he served alive. It's God's problem now. Let's get him out of here and into a cemetery as fast as we can.**

## WAKES

In the past it was customary for close friends to sit up all night with the deceased feeling horrible and creepy. That was before cocaine. Nowadays everyone has already sat up all night with the deceased feeling horrible and creepy while he was still alive.

## MORTUARY VIEWINGS

When the funeral service is conducted at a mortuary, there is usually a viewing period of several hours beforehand. Modern communications technology has had an unfortunate effect on mortuary viewings. Many people do not come to the mortuary viewing because they are under the impression that eventually the body will be sold to cable and they can see it at home later.

## BURIAL DRESS

The deceased should be buried in what he would have worn on any other somber occasion, such as a court appearance. The handcuffs can be hidden beneath the body.

## THE FUNERAL SERVICE

A funeral service resembles a wedding except it's less serious because the consequences of the ceremony are already known and there's no danger of repetition.

Ushers are used to show drunk people how to sit down feet first. Pallbearers take the place of bridesmaids. And the family follows the casket down the aisle.

The casket should be closed for Catholic and Episcopal services and open for services at which teen-age cousins are present who need to be convinced to stay off drugs.

Eulogies given by friends instead of clergymen can be less honest, and, in fact, should be if there are DEA agents in the audience.

For the service itself a very modern alternative to a priest or minister would be the deceased's accountant:

> **In the sure and certain hope of the resurrection to eternal life through our Lord Jesus Christ, we commend to Almighty God our brother Elliot; and we commit his body to the ground; earth to earth; ashes to ashes; excess personal income to tax-free municipal bonds at eleven and a half percent.**

## PALLPERSONS

In a modern funeral women as well as men may be used as pallbearers. Women, however, sometimes lack the necessary upper-body strength to carry a casket in the usual way and are therefore allowed to grab it in a leg hold.

## PROCESSION TO THE CEMETERY

The long procession of cars from the funeral to the cemetery creates that most apropos expression of modern grief, the memorial traffic jam. The drivers of the hearse and cars bearing the principal mourners should make sure to use the drive-thru window at McDonald's and not stop and park and interrupt the proceedings.

## THE BURIAL CEREMONY

The burial ceremony should be brief, especially if the widow has a dinner party to go to and needs to wash her hair. The body should be buried in the ground and not in a pile of leaves or by children with little pails and shovels at the beach.

As an alternative to burial the coffin may be cast into the sea from the deck of a ship, but not into the highway from the tailgate of a Jeep Wagoneer. That restriction is largely sanitary, however, and not governed by rules of etiquette. If you live in an area with good refuse-disposal services, you may do what you like.

## GRAVE MARKERS AND MEMORIALS

There is no reason a person's grave marker should be any quieter than his life. But the weeping angels, shrouded virgins, and holy lambs of nineteenth-century funerary sculpture

are hopelessly out of date. Some more contemporary sugges-
tions for large stone carvings are a telephone with the receiver
off the hook or a Mercedes-Benz turned upside down in its
movie-studio parking spot.

## CREMATION

Cremation allows for more creative disposition of remains.
The ashes may be scattered over the food at the deceased's
favorite restaurant, used in the litter box of his cats, or spread
on the icy driveway of a friend's ski house in place of rock salt,
which causes corrosion in automobiles and is harmful to plant-
life ecology.

## BEHAVIOR AT THE FUNERAL

The purpose of a funeral service is to comfort the living. It
is important at a funeral to display excessive grief. This will
show others how kind-hearted and loving you are and their
improved opinion of you will be very comforting.

As anyone familiar with modern fiction and motion pictures
knows, excessive grief cannot be expressed by means of tears
or a mournful face. It is necessary to break things, hit people,
and throw yourself onto the top of the coffin, at least. A really
novel way to show excessive grief is to dress up like the
deceased, go home with his parents, and insist on living with
them forever. If this seems to be too much, you can stand on
top of the floral arrangements and urinate into the open grave

while screaming, "Piss on you for dying, you asshole." Nobody will be able to argue with the strength of your emotion if you do that. The key phrase, if anyone objects, is "He would have wanted it this way." Given the amount of perversity rampant today, he may have.

## MEMORIAL SERVICES

If the deceased's friends are too dissipated to make it to any part of the funeral, it is usual to hold a memorial service at a time and place convenient to their life-styles.

The purpose of a memorial service, like that of a funeral, is to comfort the living. Therefore it is usually an affair so large, noisy, and boisterous that the deceased is hardly missed. Smaller, quieter memorial services may also be held, of course. A moment of silence might be observed, for instance, between the first time you sleep with the widow and the next time.

## MOURNING

Public display of mourning is no longer made by people of fashion, although some flashier kinds of widows may insist on sleeping with only black men during the first year after the death.

Normal social life, however, may not be resumed by a widow because there has been no normal social life in the United States since 1966.

# Section IV

## THE ENTERTAINING
## PART OF LIFE

*Let me smile with the wise and feed with the rich.*

—Samuel Johnson

# 19

## *Real Parties*

Then why should we turmoil in cares and in
    fears,
Turn all our tranquill'ty to sighs and to tears?
Let's eat, drink, and play till the worms do
    corrupt us,
      'Tis certain, Post mortem
      Nulla Voluptas.
For health, wealth and beauty, wit, learning and
    sense,
Must all come to nothing a hundred years
    hence.
                —Thomas Jordan

*A* real party differs from other social events in two ways:
1. As much as anyone can remember, it was more fun.
2. No one can remember very much.

Real parties are given for pleasure only and never to mark an occasion. There can no more be a reason for a real party than there can be an excuse for what goes on after it starts.

Real parties vary tremendously in type and style, but all share certain things in common.

- Real parties don't start until after midnight.
- No friendships or romantic relationships should survive a real party fully intact.
- Neither should much furniture.
- Someone should have underpants on his head by two A.M.
- By three A.M. someone should have called the police.
- Someone else should have called George Bush long distance to invite him over.
- By five A.M. everyone should have gotten in cars and tried to go someplace else and backed into each other instead.
- It's not a real party if it doesn't end in an orgy or a food fight.
- All your friends should still be there when you come to in the morning.

Most parties are not real parties. And some parties can never be real parties no matter how hard the partygoers try. Among these are:

- Office Christmas parties
- Wine-tasting parties
- Book-publishing parties
- Parties with themes, such as "Las Vegas Nite" or "Waikiki Whoopee"
- Parties at which anyone is wearing a blue velvet tuxedo jacket
- Parties at the homes of people who don't smoke, have subscriptions to *Commentary*, own china figurine collections, or were ever in the Peace Corps

- Parties at which more than six of the guests are related by blood
- The Republican Party

## WHERE TO HAVE A PARTY

There is only one hard-and-fast rule about the place to have a party: someone else's place.

## SMALL PARTIES

Small parties are very easy to plan. An old Supremes tape, a gram of cocaine, a fifth of Stolichnaya, and some copies of *Penthouse* from the 70s when it was really dirty make for a perfect small party without the bother and complication of guests.

## LARGE PARTIES

Large parties require much more than a gram of cocaine and, usually, other people besides yourself.

## *Whom to Invite*

- People with much more than a gram of cocaine
- All neighbors within earshot

- Everybody you've ever slept with unless he or she insists on being accompanied by a lawyer
- A lawyer of your own
- Girls who take their clothes off at the slightest provocation
- A homo to pick out the dance music
- A bunch of people who've all married each other's former husbands and wives (to get the mate-swapping mood established)
- Cute people
- Loud people
- People who get drunk fast
- Some famous people (they don't actually have to come, just be expected)
- Some Kennedys
- Some insecure people to make fools of themselves when the Kennedys show up
- At least one person who will be deeply shocked by what goes on (try not to be married to this one)

As a general rule, figure out how many people the room will hold comfortably and invite ten times that many people. Fun, like the flu, is contagious through close personal contact.

## *Whom Not to Invite*

- Andy Warhol
- Pat Robertson
- Your parents

## MUSIC

All music necessary for a real party can be supplied by a half dozen Supremes records and one dance music tape selected by the homo. Volume is more important than content anyway. Volume is everything. If the volume won't kill songbirds in the yard and make the dog wet, it's not going to be a real party.

## DANCING

Teen-agers and old people may know how to dance, but real people who go to real parties haven't the slightest. The only dances they even half remember how to do are the ones they learned twenty-five years ago. This is what the old Supremes tape is for: stiff and overweight versions of the Jerk, the Mashed Potato, the Pony, the Swim, and the Watusi. And after six drinks everyone will revert to the Twist.

Another kind of dancing that's done at real parties is the Gator, which is done only after four or five hours of partying and doesn't require any music at all. In order to do the Gator the woman should lie down and the man should lie on top of her and then they should wiggle around like gators. The best way to do this is on top of a pile of coats in the guest room.

## DISHES AND GLASSWARE

Dishes make remarkably bad Frisbees, so it doesn't matter what kind of dishes you have at a party. But the glassware must be real glass because it's impossible to get a plastic champagne goblet to break in the fireplace with anything approaching a satisfactory noise. Remember:

> *Members of the upper class*
> *Love the sound of broken glass*
> *—Maurice Baring*

It's also hard to impress anyone by taking a bite out of a paper cup. And real napkins are important, too, since blindfolding someone for kinky sex is difficult with a paper towel.

## PROFESSIONAL HELP

Professional help can be had from AA. Paraprofessional help can be gotten anywhere with all-night emergency ambulance service.

## PARTY GAMES

Most real parties are too chaotic to sustain party games. But every now and then you'll find yourself with a group of guests who are in the mood for this kind of entertainment.

## *Indoor-Outdoor Sports*

It's always amusing to play any outdoor sport indoors. Bicycle races, for instance, or motocross events if your halls and stairways are wide enough. Outdoor sports played indoors are properly played with appropriate indoor equipment. "Dog soccer" is fun; so is "ashtray tennis" and "touch footstool." Playing golf indoors with meatballs and umbrellas is invariably delightful, as is duck hunting with real guns, if you can get someone to dress up as the duck.

## *Strip Russian Roulette*

A single bullet is put into a revolver. Each player spins the cylinder and pulls the trigger. Anyone who doesn't kill himself has to remove a piece of clothing. Strip Russian roulette's combination of sex and death makes for a highly psychological game.

## *Pin the Bill on the Restaurant*

This is played when a real party is held in a tavern or other commercial establishment. The bar owner is blindfolded, spun around three times, and while he's trying to figure out what's going on, everybody runs out the door.

## *Jump Dick*

Played with a penis instead of a jump rope.

## Kick the Husband

This is usually played after the party. It is similar to kick-the-can but is played with a divorce court instead of a foot.

## PARTY DRINKS

## The Traditional Party Bar

Long-established custom decrees that the well-stocked bar for a real party should be made up of the following:

> *2 six-packs of Miller Lite*
> *1 warm keg of extremely foamy Stroh's*
> *150 half-gallon bottles of screw-top jug wine*
> *40 bottles of gin*
> *60 bottles of vodka*
> *1 bottle of tonic*
> *3 ice cubes*
> *a lime*

Tradition may be broken with, however, and other supplies added if any of the party drinks below are to be served.

## Dieter's Delight

Mix equal parts of oil and vinegar with two ounces of vodka and garnish with a leaf of romaine lettuce.

## Champagne Urbana

Domestic champagne served in a University of Illinois varsity sweater. Soak sweater in a punch bowl and wring sleeves into guests' mouths. Good for reunions and tailgate parties.

## Dinner Mint Julep

Urban variation of old southern standby. Use a small glass to crush up two chocolate-covered dinner mints in a splash of soda water. Add three ounces of bourbon, strain, and pour into Collins glass. Freshens the breath. Tic Tacs may be substituted.

## Chicken Shot

Like a bullshot but mix chicken noodle soup instead of beef bouillon with the vodka. Your Jewish friends will particularly enjoy this drink.

## Clarabell Cocktail

Fill one guest with Scotch, then squirt him in the face with a seltzer bottle. A nostalgia drink.

## Cold Buttered Rum

A hot weather drink. Put rum, cinnamon, and cloves in a twelve-ounce glass, add cider, then use hotel butter pats instead of ice cubes.

## Hamnog

Combine three ounces of brandy with a tablespoon of sugar, one cup of milk, and a half cup of crushed ice, then add sliced ham instead of an egg. Cloves, rather than nutmeg, may be grated over the top.

## Liquor Daiquiri

Women expect anything in their daiquiris except liquor. Put some booze in there instead of pineapples, mangos, peaches, or frozen bananas.

## Rum Gumbo Surprise

A bowl full of sliced okra and rum with live shrimp swimming in it.

## Whiskey Sweet and Sour

Pour three ounces of blended whiskey in a Delmonico glass and stir in Chinese food to taste.

## Zen Martini

A martini with no vermouth at all. And no gin, either.

## Sucker Punch
## Singapore Ass in a Sling
## Attica Sunrise

These are names for Gatorade and grain alcohol. Mix half and half.

## Drinks for the Dog

**You know you haven't had enough to drink yet if the dog hasn't been given a martini.**
**—The Official Preppy Desk Diary**

Unfortunately most dogs will not drink a martini. But there are a number of cocktails a dog *will* drink. Here are a few:
• Vodka and spoiled meat
• Gin and chicken gizzards
• Beer, Alpo, and dog biscuit punch

## Serving Drinks with a Garden Hose

The trick is to use one of those garden sprayer attachments made to be used with pesticide.

# *Turning Your Car Trunk into a Punch Bowl*

What a good idea. Why don't you try it?

# *How to Keep the Cocktail Onions out of the Filtration System When Making a Martini the Size of a Swimming Pool*

Use regular full-sized onions instead.

## PARTY FOOD

If it really is a real party no one will care about food. Food may still be served, however, but strictly for its amusement value.

# *Dog-Food Tartare*

Don't tell anyone the recipe until everyone has had some.

# *Hors d'Drugs*

Getting the toothpicks into the Quaaludes is the tough part.

186

## Anchovy Rolls in the Hay

Scatter a tray full of anchovy rolls under the covers in a bed that you know some couple is going to sneak off and get into

## Whale Caviar

Actually it's shelled goose eggs soft-boiled for one and a half minutes. What a mess.

## Margarine

The ideal party spread. Spread it on the guests. (Doesn't go rancid as fast as butter and the gooey sticks are more erotic than Crisco cans.)

## Pizza for Five Hundred

With everything. Have it all delivered to your boss's house or someplace like that.

## Raw Eggs

Taste terrible but are great in a food fight.

## Canned Ham on a Stick

Nothing could be easier. Take ham out of can and put a stick in it. Makes hilarious Oldenburg-type giant canapés for artsy crowd.

## Bearded Clam Dip

Best left to the imagination.

## Spaghetti as Finger Food

Secret is to use the microwave instead of boiling it.

## Soup Nagasaki

Put unopened cans of Campbell's soup into oven at five hundred degrees and get out of there, fast.

## MISCELLANEOUS HINTS AND TIPS
## FOR REAL PARTY GUESTS

### The Dignified Way to Vomit

Remain standing. With right hand, hold cocktail out to side at arm's length. Bow deeply at the waist. Include all regurgitation in one retch. Resume upright position. Use left hand to wipe mouth with handkerchief (not toilet paper). Take another drink.

### Five Amusing Places to Take a Leak

1. In someone's galoshes
2. Off the Truman balcony at the White House
3. Into the centerpiece from on top of the mantel
4. Through a keyhole
5. Out of a moving convertible (face the rear)

### Fight Etiquette

• Never fight an inanimate object.
• Never hit anyone below the belt, particularly a black one earned in karate.
• Never try to break the end off a bottle if it's plastic and disposable.

189

• Never hit anyone from behind (people should be *kicked* from behind).

• When your opponent is down, never kick him in the teeth with pointed Italian shoes. (Gentlemen do not wear pointed Italian shoes; use riding boots.)

• Remember, it's a form of social climbing to hit anyone bigger than you are.

• Never hit a woman you haven't been married to at least once. (Exceptions can be made if the marriage would have been sufficiently awful.)

• You shouldn't point a loaded gun at anyone. (This is not an absolutely rigid rule. An absolutely rigid rule is: Never, ever, point an *unloaded* gun at anyone.)

## Thank-You Notes the Next Day

If you are in any condition to write a thank-you note the next day, it wasn't a real party.

# 20

## Going Out

*We don't go anywhere. Going somewhere is for squares. We just go.*

—Marlon Brando
*The Wild One*

Going out is what you do when you don't have anything else to do. Going out is the modern equivalent of staying home alone. Unless they're on the telephone, modern people never stay home alone. This is because modern people cannot stand to be by themselves for more than fifteen minutes. There is a strong contemporary aversion to bad company.

## GOING OUT VS. DATING

Going out is not the same as dating. If you had a date you'd have someplace to go, i.e., over to the date's house to watch a rented video. Going out is normally done in packs. Packs are groups of people who would be friends if moderns had any. Going out can be combined with dating, however, if it's a nonsexual date.

## TYPES OF NONSEXUAL DATES

### The Hot Walker

A hot walker is a young and poor man who escorts an old and rich woman. The proper etiquette is for the young man to have "pretend sex" with the old woman to boost her ego. Pretend sex is just like real sex except you pretend you didn't have it.

### The Beard

A beard is a secret homosexual out on a date with a person of the opposite sex who is a secret homosexual, too. The protocol is for these two to have several more dates and then get married to perfect their heterosexual disguises.

# The Stalking Horse

A stalking horse is a person you date in order to make the person you really want to date jealous. You have to sleep with the stalking horse or the person you really want to date won't be jealous enough.

## WHERE TO GO

One problem with going out nowadays is that there's no place to go. This is the result of excessive hipness. It's no use going to a play or a movie because playwrights and movie directors are too hip for naive concepts like good and bad. But, without good and bad, it's hard to have a plot. Musicians are hip, too, and refuse to make a distinction between good drugs and bad drugs. As a result they're all dead and concerts are lousy. As for sporting events, with no good guys to root for, all the excitement has moved to the realms of union negotiations and urine testing. So there's no place to go. Not that that stops anyone from going there.

## THE MOVIES

The movies are so dull these days that the only polite thing to do is provide the entertainment yourself. After the movie starts, change seats frequently and fondle the people you sit down next to.

## THE THEATER

For modern plays especially, a nice thing to do is to create some real dramatic action. Phone in a bomb threat. Creating a real ending for a modern play is more difficult and may require a real bomb.

## OPERA

Always wear a tall silk hat to the opera because you can hide a Sony Walkman in there. Listen to *Tommy* by the Who.

## ROCK CONCERTS

The only way you can really show your appreciation for a good rock group is to put on an equally good show for them in the audience. Stand on your seat, throw bottles, and light firecrackers. Then urge everyone to make a rush for the stage. Rock stars love showy and dramatic displays of affection.

If the show wasn't any good, wait outside the stage door with a gun. This will lift the rock star's spirits by making him feel as important as John Lennon.

## SPORTING EVENTS

Whenever you go out to a sports event, it's your responsibility to make the event more fun for everyone, players and fans alike.

### *Football*

Take your cue from the pros on the field and do lots of drugs. Another thing you can do to improve the game is toss an extra ball on the field during a pileup.

### *Baseball*

Baseball is much too slow. It needs blocking. But one good thing about the way baseball players just stand there is that they make great airpistol targets.

You can also make baseball more fun by dressing as an umpire, sneaking out on the field, and giving peculiar calls.

### *Tennis*

Tennis players aren't stodgy anymore, but tennis fans are still real stick-in-the-muds. Show them how to have a good time the way college football fans do. Bring a TV and a gallon of martinis into the stands and make up loud cheers:

***Throw that racket!***
***Swear out loud!***

195

**Slap the ball boy!**
**Moon the crowd!**
**ENDORSEMENTS! ENDORSEMENTS! ENDORSEMENTS!**

After each match you should run out on the court and tear up the net.

## Basketball

The sad thing about basketball is that many of the players are embarrassed about being such tall black people. Put burnt cork on your face, wear an extra-long overcoat, and sit on the shoulders of a pal in the audience. This will make the players feel more comfortable about their appearance. Something else you can do to take their minds off their troubles is climb up, drop your trousers, and make a "pressed ham" against the clear Plexiglas backboard.

## Hockey

Hockey players are underpaid compared to many other professional athletes. Throw coins heated over your Bic lighter onto the ice to supplement their salaries.

Another problem with hockey is that it's too violent. Penalties in the penalty box should be more severe to provide deterrence. Help out by pouring beer on the players in there.

## *Olympic Sports*

The Olympics are even duller than baseball. Hire some half-naked cheerleaders for the fencing matches, walking races, and equestrian events.

## GALLERY OPENINGS

There is only one truly courteous thing to do at a gallery opening: Go straight up to the artist and write him a check for the full asking price of his most expensive work. This will make the artist feel wonderful, get the party started off with a bang, and you can stop payment the next day.

## MUSEUMS

Museums aren't festive enough. They're filled with dull, grungy Old Masters and incomprehensible modern stuff. Buy a cheerful hand-painted Elvis portrait at a local crafts fair and put a big, serious gilt frame on it with one of those little brass picture lamps at the top. Slip this into the museum and hang it in a gallery. (Museums always leave too much space between their paintings.) See how long it takes anyone to notice.

## CHIC RESTAURANTS

Just as you can enliven the atmosphere in a museum by bringing your own art, so you can enliven the atmosphere in a chic restaurant by bringing your own food and having a picnic. It's cheaper, too.

## CHIC NEW RESTAURANTS

Chic *new* restaurants require different behavior from well-established watering holes. New restaurants need lots of publicity if they're going to thrive. Try to get them some by throwing drinks at celebrity patrons or driving your car right through the place.

## CHURCH

Church wouldn't seem to be a very interesting place to go. But that's not true. All sorts of perfectly normal activities— drinking, dope smoking, love-making—are somehow terrifically exciting when done in a church. Even a fart can be wonderfully entertaining if it happens in a confessional booth: "Forgive me, Father, for I have . . ."

## DANCE CLUBS

A dance club is the one place you should never go when you're going out. Dance clubs should be reserved for business only. Palladium, Vertigo, Limelight, and so on are terrible places for partying, but they are wonderful places to give dictation to a secretary or to have life insurance salesmen meet you after work.

## THE CIRCUS

What with the number of clowns, wild animals, and people doing death-defying acts that we all know already, there's no reason on earth to visit the circus. Visit your friends instead. They are almost certain not to serve you boiled peanuts in the shell.

## PARTY CRASHING

Walk right in and loudly announce how rude it was that you weren't invited. It is the duty of those with good manners to instruct the less fortunate.

# Section V

## THAT PART OF LIFE
## WHICH IS NOT IN THE
## LEAST ENTERTAINING

*O Duty,*
*Why hast thou not the visage of a sweetie or a*
*cutie?*
*Why displayest thou the countenance of the kind*
*of conscientious organizing spinster*
*That the minute you see her you are aginster?*
*Why glitter thy spectacles so ominously?*
*Why art thou clad so abominously?*
*Why art thou so different from Venus?*
*And why do thou and I have so few interests*
*mutually in common between us?*

—Ogden Nash

# 21

# Courtesy in the Workplace

*Th' old story iv th' ant an' th' grasshopper—th'
ant that ye can step on an' the' grasshopper ye
can't catch.*

—Finley Peter Dunne

$\mathcal{A}$nyone who has good manners on the job probably won't have that job long. Courtesy does not belong in the workplace. The only thing jobs have to do with etiquette is that it's polite to have a good one and rude to have a bad one.

## GETTING A GOOD JOB: BACKGROUND AND TRAINING

Skills are an important factor in obtaining a good job. George Mitchell, for example, does not have any skills. He can't weld, lay brick, type, or take dictation. As a result George Mitchell had to look for work someplace where skills were not important, and today he is majority leader of the Senate. Avoid learning useful skills and you'll have a chance to turn out like George Mitchell. But go to dental school, and you'll drill teeth for the rest of your life.

Prestigious educational institutions are a good place to avoid learning useful skills. They're also valuable for the friends you'll meet there. At least six of the twelve Disciples would never have been able to get jobs as saints if they hadn't attended exclusive religious instruction with the likes of Peter, bishop of Rome, and John the Evangelist.

Good schools are worthwhile, too, for the enormous amount of spare time you'll have when you aren't studying. And you never have to study at a good school, because it's so impressive to say, "I flunked out of Harvard." But if you say, "I got straight A's at Wayne State," who cares?

Use that spare time to get romance out of your system by being wildly promiscuous. There's no worse career disadvantage than being married to the first person you had a crush on as a youth. Margaret Trudeau made this mistake. She married Pierre when she was twenty-two; then he got older and became prime minister of Canada, and it nearly wrecked her career of dancing without underpants in discothèques.

204

## CHOOSING A FIELD

Once you have the right kind of background, the next step in getting a good job is to pick a field of employment. This is easy because there's only one industry left in the United States: entertainment. Everything else is manufactured in East Asia. So far, however, Singapore, South Korea, and Japan have not been able to develop a cheaper, better made, and technologically more sophisticated *All My Children*.

There are plenty of job opportunities in entertainment. Entertainment is a broad field. It covers not only singing, dancing, producing, and directing but also running for political office, large-scale financial embezzling, national-security advising, the messier kinds of divorcing, and being self-aggrandizing president of a huge obsolete corporation the way Lee Iacocca is.

In the entertainment industry's best jobs, what you're paid to do is be famous. Getting these jobs can be tricky because one of the qualifications is to be famous already. However, any kind of fame will do. You can be famous for being sick all the time, like Marcel Proust. You can be famous for being dull-normal, like Gerald Ford. In fact, you can be famous for having nothing to be famous for, like Joey Bishop.

Probably the easiest way to become famous is to be responsible for a lot of people getting killed. This is what got Dwight Eisenhower the presidency, Henry Kissinger a huge book contract, and Charles Manson on the cover of *Life* magazine. Eisenhower and Kissinger did better with this tactic than Manson, but they had ironclad alibis about what they were doing during D-Day and the Cambodia incursion.

# THE JOB INTERVIEW

When going on a job interview, do not pretend to be a handicapped black woman. Corporations are only kidding when they say they are equal-opportunity employers. Also, unless you really *are* a handicapped black woman, you're going to look silly with cordovan shoe polish all over your face, wearing a dress, and sitting in a wheelchair you don't know how to operate.

It's much better to come to a job interview dressed in a subdued manner. Try to present a conservative and competent image of yourself. Keep in mind what kind of person is going to be interviewing you. It'll probably be a male in his late thirties or early forties who's just recently risen to the position of personnel manager. He'll be conservative and competent himself, and he's going to want to hire people who are the same way, because that's his job. But don't forget that twenty years ago this personnel manager was wearing his hair like Chewbacca, gobbling psilocybin mushrooms, and throwing ox blood on draft files. When he sees you trying to present a conservative and competent image, deep in his heart he's going to think you're a dweeb. You can get around this by waiting until the end of the interview and then leaning across his desk and saying in a confidential manner, "Sure, I'm conservative and competent, but, just between you and me, if they reinstitute compulsory military service, I am going to feel morally obligated to dress up like a circus clown, get addicted to drugs, and shoot cops." He'll dig it, and you'll get the job.

## STARTING AT THE BOTTOM

Once you've been offered employment, insist on starting at the bottom. People are forever rising from the mail room to become heads of giant corporations. But no one has ever risen from junior management trainee to become head of anything. A junior-management trainee gets to see the boss about once a year, in a staff meeting. But if you're delivering mail, you'll see the chairman of the board every day and will have a much better chance of catching him snorting blow off his desk blotter or, better, trying to fondle you.

Also, with your prestigious educational-institution background and murder-case notoriety, you'll shine compared to the members of disadvantaged minorities working with you in the mail room, who have only a few assault-and-battery convictions to their credit. Promotions should come fast.

## CAREER ADVANCEMENT

The most important way to assure career advancement is to be helpful. If someone has too much to do, help him out. Maybe you'll have a coworker who has completed five or six very successful projects. He probably won't have time to take credit for all of them. Help him out.

207

## ADVICE

As you attain higher levels of corporate responsibility, you'll start getting a lot of advice about how to do your job better. Some of this will be good advice, like "Get in early, stay late, and take an eight-hour lunch." But most of it will be worthless. For instance, one current piece of wisdom in management technique is to emulate the Japanese. But walking around Manhattan as part of a large group of people wearing white socks, nodding furiously, and taking pictures of Rockefeller Center will probably not help your career. It's much better to improve your job performance by using methods you already understand, such as taking drugs.

Take a different drug every day to help you determine what kind of on-the-job behavior will be most valuable to you. If your work goes well while you're taking Methedrine, you have a job requiring verbal assertiveness that doesn't have to make much sense. Methedrine is a perfect drug for the public-relations field.

If you find it easier to be drunk, then your job requires *physical* assertiveness that doesn't have to make *any* sense, such as shaping U.S. foreign policy.

When marijuana produces the best results, your job calls for a mellow, laid-back, low-pressure style. In recessionary times, this probably means your company is about to go out of business.

And if cocaine seems to be the best-working drug for you, you've probably got employment in a hip, with-it field like contemporary comedy. It's hard to stay hip and with-it all the time. Maybe you should try something even more hip, like heroin. Or mix the two together and get a job as a dead legend.

## SELF-EMPLOYMENT

If you're unable to find any kind of job, there's always the option of self-employment. One increasingly popular type of self-employment is suing people. You can sue anybody for anything, and there are plenty of out-of-work lawyers urging you to do so. You'll find it easy to injure yourself by shoving Sony Walkman earphones down your throat, sticking your tongue into the back of a video arcade game, trying to run your foot through a pasta-making machine, or doing any number of other oddball things with the products of major manufacturers. And all these people are liable. This is how Ralph Nader has made a living for years.

Or, perhaps you can start your own retail business. It should be something that doesn't require a lot of expensive machinery, perhaps in the personal-service field. You probably already know how to do something that involves interaction with other people that you could turn a profit on. No doubt there is a career opportunity right in your lap, so to speak. Feel around down there. You've got it.

## THE FRUITS OF SUCCESS

Once you have a good job and lots of money and power, good manners will follow as a matter of course. You'll be able to act as rudely as you want and still contribute to making the world a more courteous place because of how polite and nice everybody will be to you.

# 22

## Social Correspondence

" 'Except of me Mary my dear as your
walentine and think over what I've said.—My
dear Mary I will now conclude.' That's all," said
Sam.
"That's rather a sudden pull-up, ain't it,
Sammy?" inquired Mr. Weller.
"Not a bit on it," said Sam; "she'll vish there
wos more, and that's the great art o' letter-
writin'."

—Charles Dickens
*The Pickwick Papers*

Unfortunately the great art
of letter writing has fallen into complete disuse, replaced by
the great art of apologizing to angry parents and erstwhile

hostesses for enormous long-distance bills run up on their phones.

## MODERN LETTERS

Letters nowadays are used only for business purposes—usually by the phone company, threatening to cut off service. The proper way to answer such letters is to call up and say the check is lost in the mail.

## POSTCARDS

Although no one writes letters anymore, postcards are still very popular.

The correct postcard has something obscene or immensely stupid on the pictorial side but confines itself only to the stupid on the reverse or message side. A proper postcard message contains the following:

1. Cute salutation
2. Comment on the weather at the place of posting
3. Comment on the people at the place addressed
4. Closing so abbreviated as to give no indication of who sent the thing

# THE FORMAL POSTCARD

When a phone call is impractical (for instance, when you're paying for it yourself), a postcard can be employed for any purpose that the formal letter used to fulfill. For instance, the postcard of condolence:

**Dear Bubblehead,**
   **Swell weather here! Bet you're sick of snow! Sorry your daughter died in a car wreck.**
Ciao,<br>Us

# 23

# Guests, Including Pets and Old Friends from College

*"You see, they had asked me down to shoot, and
I'm not particularly immense at that sort of
thing. . . . And they tried to rag me in the
smoking-room about not being able to hit a bird
at five yards. . . . So I got up the next morning
. . . and hunted up the most conspicuous thing
in the bird line I could find, and measured the
distance, as nearly as it would let me, and shot
away. . . . I got a gardener-boy to drag it into
the hall . . . where everyone must see it on their
way to the breakfast room. I breakfasted
upstairs myself. I gathered afterwards that the*

*meal was tinged with a very unchristian spirit.*
*I suppose it's unlucky to bring peacock's*
*feathers into a house. . . ."*

—Saki
"Reginald on House-Parties"

*T*he first rule of having guests is to make sure they are comfortable. Guests are most comfortable in their own room, which is back where they came from. If they can't be convinced to go there, maybe you can convince them to go to a hotel. They should pay for the hotel room themselves. This way they'll be extra comfortable because not only won't they feel cramped but they won't feel guilty either.

The guests you're interested in seeing can all afford hotel rooms anyway. Other guests tend to be old friends from college. Benjamin Franklin said, "Fish and visitors smell in three days," but old friends from college usually smell already. Answer the door with a towel over your face and say it isn't you and you aren't home and that you don't live there besides.

## PETS

A pet is just another kind of guest and should be treated accordingly. As with human guests, it's always nicest if they sleep and go to the bathroom outside the house.

Pets are more intelligent than old friends from college, and

214

some pets can be trained to bring you your slippers instead of herpes.

## THE CAT: TODAY'S DOG

Cats are to dogs what modern people are to the people we used to have. Cats are slimmer, cleaner, more attractive, disloyal, and lazy. It's easy to understand why the cat has eclipsed the dog as modern America's favorite pet. People like pets to possess the same qualities they do. Cats are irresponsible and recognize no authority, yet are completely dependent on others for their material needs. Cats cannot be made to do anything useful. Cats are mean for the fun of it. In fact, cats possess so many of the same qualities as some people (expensive girlfriends, for instance) that it's often hard to tell the people and the cats apart.

## How to Tell a Cat from an Expensive Girlfriend

- If it goes to the bathroom under the sink, it's probably a cat.
- If it wants jewelry, it's probably a girlfriend.
- Girlfriends will not usually eat horsemeat (unless the restaurant has an extremely chic reputation).

# HOUSEPLANTS

The houseplant has become America's second most popular pet. This is also easy to understand. Houseplants are even more like modern people than cats are. Houseplants are on strict low-calorie diets and spend most of their time waiting to bloom.

# BEING A GUEST YOURSELF

When going to visit your own old friends from college, be sure to show up unannounced in the middle of the night. Not much is going on in the middle of the night and your hosts are probably bored. Remember to bring a present for the hostess. A practical or attractive present is too old-fashioned. The most popular modern present to bring is a whole bunch of other people who want to stay there, too. Otherwise, a bouquet of hard drugs or a live monkey is nice.

Make a loud continuous party out of your visit. Try to stay a lifetime. And don't insult your hosts by giving them money for the food and liquor you consume. They aren't running a hotel, after all. Return their hospitality instead by inviting them to stay with someone else they know.

It's a nice touch, when you're a houseguest, to make your bed. It's a particularly nice touch to make it a place of delight for your host's teen-age daughters.

## A TIP FOR CAT LOVERS: DON'T GIVE YOUR PET COCAINE

Twenty years ago it was fashionable to blow marijuana smoke in your cat's face and watch it "get mellow." This was fine for marijuana. Do not, however, give your cat cocaine. If you do, it will climb the wallpaper, shred the drapes, and tear apart every piece of furniture in the house looking for catnip so it can get to sleep. Then it will spend the night howling in the backyard, and, after you've passed out, will sneak back in the house and take all the rest of your cocaine.

For the same reason do not give cocaine to other animals. In particular, do not give cocaine to animals that aren't there, such as the giant spiders you think you see under the couch.

# 24

# *The Servants*

*Vivre? Les serviteurs feront cela pour nous.*
        —Philipe Auguste Villiers
            De L'Isle-Adam

*U*ntil recently a prosperous family employed a housekeeper to superintend the general domestic establishment: a butler to take charge of the dining room, pantry, and parlor floor; footmen to answer the door and assist in serving the table; a valet and lady's maid to attend to the personal needs of the master and mistress of the house; parlor maids, kitchen maids, and chambermaids to do the cleaning; a gardener to tend the grounds; a cook to prepare meals; a chauffeur to drive the car; and a nurse and a governess to care for the children. Today all these functions are combined in the single person of the cleaning lady who comes in once a week. What she does is a little dusting.

Before the cleaning lady arrives, it is necessary to vacuum the entire house and straighten up all the rooms, because she works for friends of yours the other six days of the week and you don't want her to tell them how you really live. Be especially careful about hiding drug paraphernalia, sex toys, and the like. And get any unusual or alarming bedmates out of there before she comes.

It is perfectly proper to ask your cleaning lady to iron, wash windows, polish silver, do the grocery shopping, and clean up after the dog. You can also ask her to jump through a flaming hoop with a cold leg of mutton in her mouth for all the good it will do you. She's going to dust a little, and that's it, no matter what.

It is also considered quite proper to yell at your cleaning lady, allow your children to do the same, threaten to report her to the immigration authorities, and give her a lot of worthless and condescending advice about what to do with her husband the drunk. A cleaning lady is somebody who really violates your personal space, so it's not bad manners to treat her poorly. She'll understand. And she'll reciprocate by not considering it bad manners to steal money from you to bring her salary up to half of the minimum wage.

# 25

# Real Trouble

*Send lawyers, guns, and money,*
*The shit has hit the fan.*

—Warren Zevon

Real trouble is not the same as acting up or being intentionally rude. Real trouble results in death or a long prison term.

Nothing could be more modern or more mannerly than real trouble. It produces that rarest and most exquisite contemporary sensation—the polite thrill.

# THE LACK OF POLITE THRILLS IN MODERN LIFE

With the elimination of social complexities, such as duty and virtue, modern life has come to be guided only by the pursuit of pleasure and the avoidance of pain. Thus humans have attained the same natural perfection as wild beasts. But a price has been paid for this honest simplicity. Without the pricks of conscience or obligations of rectitude to force us into dangers, our lives are no more thrilling than the lives of beetle larvae. Real trouble fixes this.

If the lady next door roasts her child—preheating the oven to 550 degrees and placing the baby, fat side up, on a rack in an open pan, reducing the heat immediately to 350 degrees and cooking eighteen to twenty minutes per pound until dead—numerous thrills are provided. There is the thrill of violent sensation (especially if you happen to open the oven door yourself). There is the thrill of importance as you carry the news to others, and the thrill of creativity as you invent things about your neighbor to tell the newspapers. And, most important, there is the ultimate, fabulous, and very polite thrill of not having given in to the temptation to do this to your own kid.

But it is this very thrill of *not* having caused the pandemonium that points out the one big problem with real trouble: It's such a bore waiting for others to get into it. Waiting goes against the impatient grain of modern life. As a result, many people feel compelled to get into real trouble themselves even though they know it's going to be a bother.

# GETTING INTO REAL TROUBLE

In order to be perfectly correct, when you decide to get into real trouble, you should make sure that it's you who gets killed or sent to jail. But etiquette is not as exacting on this point as it once was. Today it's often considered acceptable to have lots of people go to the grave or Leavenworth with you.

You must still be careful about motive, however. It shouldn't look as though you *need* to cause trouble to attract attention. It's always rude to remind others of inadequacies, especially your own.

And you should never cause trouble out of anger. If you are mad at someone and you shoot him, real trouble will result. But you'll also lose that person's friendship. The more courteous thing to do would be to slap him with a huge lawsuit. That way you'll enjoy the trouble and he'll enjoy the publicity. Thus the wheels of polite society are oiled.

Nor should you ever create trouble for a "cause." Planting pipe bombs is no end of fun, but planting them in order, say, to free Croatia from Yugoslav political control looks too calculating. Also, having a cause gives others impolite thoughts about how empty your life must be otherwise.

# TYPES OF REAL TROUBLE

## Self-Destruction

The old-fashioned way to get into real trouble was by eating, drinking, taking drugs, getting diseases, and acting like a pig and a fool until you died. Today this is considered hopelessly poky and selfish. A clearly willful act of suicide in early youth is preferable, and more interesting to the public. You should consider the feelings of others before you commit suicide. Try to kill yourself in a public place. Climb up on a bridge or out on a window ledge so that crowds can gather and cheer your urge to jump. Let at least one policeman climb out after you before you leap. This is how they get medals and promotions.

If you are too shy or too afraid of heights for such a public exit, you can include others in your gesture by leaving a well-composed suicide note. Even better is to leave a number of notes addressed to various people, explaining how each of them was the principal cause of your despair. They'll be more flattered as to their importance than they would be if included in a general "everybody hates me" sort of explanation.

Guns are always the best method for a private suicide. They are more stylish looking than single-edged razor blades and natural gas has gotten so expensive. Drugs are too chancy. You might miscalculate the dosage and just have a good time. Or you might wind up in the hospital as a human vegetable. In which case you'll spend the rest of your life being pestered to become the head of a Federal regulatory agency.

Some people favor committing suicide in the nude for additional shock value. But try to be honest with yourself about how your body looks naked. It's safer to wear something simple in white or light gray. Both go well with blood. And be sure to empty your bladder and bowels before shooting yourself. Gore from a bullet wound is very dramatic but there's always an element of low comedy to excrement (as witnessed by the mention of it throughout this book).

There are times and places, of course, where it would be very bad manners to commit suicide.

• Never commit suicide at someone else's funeral. This is stealing the show—much too pushy. The British did a lot to improve manners on the Indian subcontinent when they put a stop to *suttee*.

• Try not to kill yourself in a way that will result in your being made a martyr. The world does not need more hideous portraits printed on black velvet of the type seen depicting Martin Luther King, Jr., Jesus Christ, and John F. Kennedy.

• Do not commit suicide to get back at your parents if they actually *do* detest you. You'll just be playing into their hands.

• Young people should not kill themselves over college grades until their final exam scores have lowered the class curve.

## Murder/Suicide

More thrilling than the simple suicide is the suicide where a bunch of people are killed first. Try to pick people that you know. There's something vulgar about killing strangers. This is why polite people were so careful to dodge the draft during the war in Vietnam.

The rules for killing people are similar to the rules for having houseguests, except, instead of doing everything you can to make people comfortable, you should do everything you can to make them dead.

Only a very rude host would serve himself first. By the same token, only a very rude murderer/suicide would kill himself first.

Try to kill people quickly. It's just as inconsiderate to

torture people to death as it is torture them with a long, boring story about your psychiatric problems.

## Killing Strangers

With the use of tact and consideration, killing strangers can be made less vulgar, even socially acceptable. For instance, when sniping from the top of a building, try to pick people who seem to be having a bad day anyhow. And never commit only one murder. You wouldn't serve a meal with only one course. Frankly, it is common.

Remember to think visually. If you commit your murders at all well, there'll be a movie made about them. Out of consideration for the producer, you want that movie to be a hit. Do your killing someplace with interesting scenery and pick victims with colorful personalities or who resemble famous actors. It also helps if you give yourself a nickname that can be used as the movie title. "The Earmuff Murderer," "The Six-Inch Naval Gun Killer," "The Silly Strangler," and "The Sock-in-the-Mouth Suffocater" are several possibilities.

## Bombs

There is something impersonal about bombs that keeps them from ever being in the best of taste. An exception is if you are the head of government in a country with an extensive nuclear arsenal. In which case you can be confident that your bombs will affect everyone in a deeply personal manner, and you may use them at will.

## *Hostage Taking*

Taking hostages is the reverse of having old friends from college come to stay at your house. When you take hostages, you've got a bunch of unpleasant, grumpy, half-crazed people on your hands, and you're threatening to shoot them if they *do* leave. This makes no sense. And a polite person wouldn't have anything to do with people as disheveled and silly-acting as most hostages, anyway.

*Pretending* to take hostages, however, is a great way to get rid of those old friends from college. Call the police and say you're holding your old friends from college at gunpoint. The police will then do everything they can to get them off your hands.

## *Sexual Assault*

Sexual assault is very outré. The better class of people are surfeited with sex and would never think of attacking anyone to get more of it (though they might hit someone over the head to get a dinner invitation).

Sexual assault is still fashionable, however, when women rape men. The literal meaning of rape is "to carry away." That is exactly how most women make their assaults—by carrying away lots of expensive clothing and jewelry from department stores and clobbering their husbands with the bill. But this is not real trouble; it's not even against the law.

## *Polite Crime*

Never forget that the purpose of real trouble is the entertainment of others. There should be something novel and unique about the trouble you get into. Your crime needs what newspapermen call a "hook."

• Stake someone out at the top of the bell tower at San Juan Capistrano and let them get fluttered to death during the annual return of the swallows.

• Cause cancer in a kidnap victim by force-feeding him refined sugar and foods with chemical preservatives in them.

• Work at an abortion clinic for ten years, then go to a Catholic country and insist on turning yourself in to the authorities as a mass murderer. (Call up the *Guinness* people, too. After ten years of giving abortions, you've probably got their mass-murderer world record.)

• Cause an anorexic girlfriend to drown by leaving the toilet seat up at her house.

• Chain-saw murder has already been done, but nobody has killed anyone yet with one of those string-fed lawn trimmers. It might take a while, but it will make the papers.

## ACCIDENTAL REAL TROUBLE

Never get into real trouble by mistake. Plane crashes, car wrecks, and accidents while cleaning guns are all too impromptu for even the casual social life of today. People will tell each other, "When something like that happens there's just nothing you can say." How true. And how boring. If you're going to have a surprise mishap, try to be beaten to death by teen-agers in the restroom of a public park that's known as a hangout for homosexuals. This will give everyone lots to say, especially your wife and children.

The value of planning cannot be overestimated. If you are going to get into real trouble, you should start laying the groundwork early in life by being quiet, shy, a straight-A student, and a dutiful child to your parents. It gives no end of pleasure to everyone when a person like that throws a flaming bucket of gasoline into the Senate from the visitors' gallery.

## THE CONSEQUENCES OF REAL TROUBLE

### Trials

If you're not killed immediately when you get into real trouble, you'll have to stand trial.

Think of the jury as your friends. That way you'll be prepared when they fuck you over.

Society holds trials for the same reason that Shakespeare had comic relief in Macbeth. So try to make everyone laugh. Pleading innocent is usually the best way to do this.

Also be sure to take the stand yourself. You wouldn't care to go to a Broadway play at which the star stayed in his dressing room while a paid expert explained his part to the audience.

And plea bargaining is tasteless—too much like being engaged in trade.

228

## Real Trouble

Always dress for a trial in a manner that shows you to be a sophisticated person. You don't want people in the court to think you ran your parents through a laundry mangle out of ignorance and stupidity.

## Prison

If the jury comes to feel they really know and understand you, you'll have to spend some time in prison. Being in prison is just like being a guest at a large house party except that you'll be sexually ravished without hints over cocktails first.

Be sure to tip the help. If you tip them to what some of the other guests are up to, you may get an early parole. Or a sharpened spoon-handle between the ribs. Either way your visit will be briefer.

## Death Sentence

If you live in a state with capital punishment, try to think up something piquant to say on your way to the gas chamber. "See you in hell, Mom," is nice. Things like "My only regret is that I have but one life to give for my country" or "Don't stop to mourn, organize" sound too stiff for what's basically an informal situation.

# Section VI

## CLOTHING

*. . . sitting, and clothed, and in his right mind . . .*
—Mark 5:15

# 26

## Men's Clothes

*A man's tie should never be louder than his
wife.*

—John Hughes

## HOW TO DRESS IN A POLITE WAY

The most polite thing in the
world is to be rich. There is nothing you can do that is more
courteous and mannerly. But, as with all points of etiquette,
appearances are everything. If you can't bring yourself to
actually *be* wealthy, the least you can do is look that way.

Therefore, any man with good manners always dresses as though he had lots of money.

Dressing like a rich man is not, however, a matter of wearing flashy and expensive clothes. Life is not that simple. Everyone wants what he doesn't have. Everyone enjoys pretending to be what he isn't. It's *poor men* who wear flashy and expensive clothes, pretending to have money. Rich men wear sturdy and practical clothes, pretending to have brains. Thus, if you want people to think you're wealthy, don't dress rich, dress smart. Besides, rich men didn't get rich in the first place by wasting good money on meringue-colored suits with shoulders as wide as the Panama Canal.

## THE RULES OF DRESSING RICH

"Don't be flashy" is the first rule of dressing rich, but there are hundreds of other rules that rich people dress by. Rich people like rules. This is probably because rules (such as the rule "Robbery is against the law") are what keep them rich.

## SHOES

Rich white Protestant men have held on to some measure of power in America almost solely by getting women, blacks, and other disadvantaged groups to wear crippling foot fashions. This keeps them too busy with corns and bunions to compete in the job market. Make sure your shoes are plain and roomy.

Black, brown, and oxblood wing tips, Oxfords, and slip-ons are excellent. But don't get plain and roomy shoes mixed up with "sensible shoes." It shouldn't look as though you have to be on your feet all day working. Construction boots, ripple-soled shoes, and anything the mailman wears are not rich. Neither are galoshes or rubbers, which show you're too poor to buy new shoes if your old ones get ruined. Also avoid great big boat-sized policeman's shoes. Whether they love rules or not, the rich are no more honest than the rest of us, and policemen make them nervous.

White shoes are very rich looking, but they have to be the completely impractical suede kind, not shiny white imitation leather. It's a general rule of wealth that if something can be wiped clean with a damp cloth, rich people can afford to throw it away.

A current rich shoe favorite is the black tassel loafer. Powerful and important men enjoy the reassuring snap of the little tassel ends. It's like having their feet report for duty every time they take a step. Don't be fooled into buying loafers with little things across the instep, however. If you really were rich you'd know that those are snaffle bits, and they belong in the mouth of your horse, not on top of your feet.

## SOCKS

The two principal types of rich socks are itchy black wool socks and itchy white wool socks. Rich people wear itchy socks so that people trying to act rich or people who just became rich and aren't used to it will be scratching all the time and give themselves away.

The black socks have to be the long, over-the-calf kind because shorter ones might not itch enough. Black socks are worn with all dress clothes and some sportswear. Other sportswear is worn with no socks. Thus rich people's white socks are never worn at all. This makes them happy. Rich people like things to last.

## NECKTIES

The single most vital piece of rich apparel is the necktie. Rich men judge each other solely on the basis of neckties. This saves a lot of small talk and résumé reading. Certain neckties say, "I'm smart" (meaning, of course, "I'm rich"). People who are are actually smart wear orange short-sleeve shirts with plastic pen shields in the pocket, make eighteen thousand dollars a year designing electronic circuitry, and don't know from neckties—which shows what brains will get you.

The rich like neckties that reflect the way they want the world to be: conservative, orderly, and strangling *you* around the neck. So never loosen your necktie in front of a rich man, or he'll think you're a liberal Democrat.

Your necktie should not be so wide that it looks as though you can't afford to get soup on your shirt. And it shouldn't be so narrow that you could get it confused with the fettuccine and accidentally wrap it around your fork and make a real fool of yourself during a business lunch. Never wear a necktie with a pattern that resembles a road map, a pizza, or a Parcheesi board. And never wear a tie made of polyester synthetics.

Rich people own oil wells. They want to get the most out of that oil. They want to see their oil used in expensive gasoline, not cheap neckties. Also avoid regimental stripes. If you hang around with rich people, sooner or later you're going to run into someone who was in that regiment. He may not care to be reminded of his war record.

A silk tie with a small repeated game-bird motif is good. This shows you are affluent enough to purchase an expensive shotgun and mean enough to use it. Rich people respect things like that. Be sure to know what the birds are, however. Don't confuse a pheasant with a duck. And if you have a duck on your necktie, make sure it isn't Daffy or Donald.

## DRESS SHIRTS

The proper dress shirt is always long sleeved with either plain cuffs and a button-down collar or French cuffs and a regular collar. It should be all cotton or look as though it is. White shirts are best, but there is a short list of conservative colors and patterns that are also acceptable: blue, pale yellow, and blue stripes on a white background. Interestingly, pink—atrociously lower class in hats, suits, cars, and politics—is considered conservative in a dress shirt. But the rich may be pulling our leg about that one.

Anyway, the really important difference between the shirts of the wealthy and the shirts of the rest of us is not their material or color but how they wear out. An ordinary man's dress shirt frays at the front of the collar from buttoning and unbuttoning and friction with polyester neckties. A rich man's shirt frays at the back of the collar because that's where the head and neck rub when the nose is pointed disdainfully in the air. You can achieve the same effect by running some fine-grit sandpaper along this part of your shirts.

Don't bother about whether the shirt goes with your tie or suit. Remember, you're supposed to be smart and have too much on your mind to bother about things like that.

## SUITS

The only suits that ever fit as badly as expensive hand-tailored Ivy League suits were the bottom-of-the-line suits from Robert Hall. It's a shame they went out of business. Other cheap suits will do, though, as long as they're the right color and fit like a canvas duffel bag.

The right colors are navy blue and dark gray, either plain or with a white stripe in them. There is, however, a complex symbolic code associated with the width and spacing of these stripes. Some stripes say "banker" or "lawyer" or "usually reliable State Department source," but other stripes say "corrupt politician," "loan shark," or "Moline farm-equipment salesman on a toot in Chicago." Most rich men have to flunk twice to stay in Yale long enough to learn the code. Stick with plain colors.

Summer suits are another matter. They can be olive, tan, khaki, light blue, dark blue, seersucker, pin cord, or a dozen other things. (Although you should never wear a white suit unless your office is in the middle of a tennis court.) Just make sure your summer suits are rumpled. Suits are not dress-up clothes for rich people. They are an everyday uniform and are treated as casually as you'd treat a pair of bib overalls and dry-cleaned about as often. Wad up your summer suits, and put them under your mattress every night.

## SPORT COATS

The rich are the only people in the world who actually wear sport coats to play sports in. So don't wear a tweed jacket to work unless you expect to flush a covey of quail from behind the Xerox machine. The only exception is the blue blazer, which is a rich man's way of saying, "I'm going straight from the office to my boat and won't have time to change."

## PANTS

One of the simplest things about dressing rich is picking out pants. Your pants should be the same as the rest of your suit. This is not true with a blue blazer, of course—blue flannel pants with big patch pockets and brass buttons would look silly.

Dark-gray pants go with a blue blazer in the winter and khaki or white pants in the summer. There's a strict rule about white pants, though. White pants should be worn only between Memorial Day and Labor Day unless you want to be mistaken for a male nurse. (The same rule holds true for white shoes and for going without socks, even though male nurses usually *do* wear socks.)

Rich men also wear certain very gaudy types of summer pants. But the code concerning these is even more complex than the suit-stripe code. There is a shade of lime-green, for instance, which indicates you're a senator from Massachusetts having a weekend affair with a movie actress on Nantucket. And there is another shade of lime-green that means you're the assistant pro-shop stock boy at a second-rate country club in Ohio. Red pants are the same way. It's very rich-looking to wear red pants, but they have to be precisely the right tone of Breton red and purchased at a particular store on Block Island that's only open two months out of the year. Some details of dressing rich are best left to the authentically wealthy.

## UNDERWEAR

Always wear boxer shorts. Never wear Jockey-style underwear or bikini briefs. It's not known why rich men wear boxer shorts, but it may be to show the world that they're too blasé to get sudden erections in public places or too rich and powerful to have to hide them.

## SPORTSWEAR

The sportswear of the rich is utilitarian and to the point. Izod tennis shirts are used for playing tennis, not for showing off pectoral muscles or cruising gay bars. By the same token, boaters are donned to go boating, polo coats are worn at polo matches, and sweaters are actually sweated in. As a result, the sweaters of the rich are always in appalling condition.

Rich men don't go in for exotic sportswear such as special shoes to run in—they have people to do their running for them. Any rubber-soled shoes are considered good enough for everything that doesn't require spikes or spurs on the feet. The exception is the leather lace-up Sperry Top-Sider moccasin. If you want to pretend you are on the America's Cup team, drag these behind your car all winter to get the correct salt-stained look. Drag your sweaters, too, if you want to look rich in those.

## JEANS AND T-SHIRTS

Never wear jeans and T-shirts. The rich associate jeans and T-shirts with unskilled manual labor. The phenomenon of designer jeans and expensive T-shirts only serves to remind the rich of how deplorably high the minimum wage has become.

## OUTERWEAR

The proper wealthy overcoat is the long, dark, straight-tailored Chesterfield, an item of apparel that not only sounds but also looks as though you're wearing a davenport. Besides being ugly, it is much too expensive for anybody who's faking it. You'll have to make do with the second-string coat of the rich, the tan trench coat.

Rich men favor the trench coat over the car coat or raincoat because they can afford dry cleaners who always lose the belt and men's stores which don't carry replacement belts so that a new trench coat has to be purchased every time an old trench coat goes to be cleaned. Incidentally, this is almost never. Rich people do not feel middle-class compulsions about cleanliness. Cleanliness may be the most important thing next to godliness, but they both take a backseat to money.

The rich also like trench coats because of the military connotation. Rich men would like to be thought of not only as smart but brave. A very important detail about trench coats is that the belt ends should be tied together, not buckled. When those howitzer shells start coming in, you don't have time to carefully buckle your trench-coat belt, but it would look as though you were frightened if you ran for cover with your coattails flying in the wind.

Don't carry an umbrella with a trench coat. That would be redundant. Not that trench coats are waterproof; they aren't. But the original ones made in World War I were, and the rich are sticklers for tradition.

Don't wear a hat, either. Rich men have given up hats for the same reason the rest of us have: They're forever losing them. You have to be a pimp to have enough women around all the time to always find your hat for you. This is, in fact, why pimps still happen to wear hats. Being a pimp is not the kind of image a rich man cares to project.

When you do carry an umbrella, don't carry the fold-up kind. Carry a long, furled black one with a canelike handle. But don't grasp the handle as though the umbrella *were* a cane. Hold the umbrella by the straight shaft below the crook as though it were a fencing foil. The rich were taking fencing while the rest of us were taking gym.

# AN EIGHT-PIECE WARDROBE THAT ALLOWS YOU TO DRESS LIKE A RICH MAN EVEN IF YOU HAVE ABSOLUTELY NO MONEY AT ALL

## 1. *Dark-Gray Pants*

These can be as old and cheap as you like and made out of any material so long as it doesn't have a slick sheen. (The rich do not want the public thinking of them as, in any way, slippery. It might result in stricter tax laws.) Make sure these pants are narrow at the bottom, have sloppy cuffs, are too short, and don't fit. This is the way Italian tailors at Brooks Brothers get revenge on their stuck-up customers.

## 2. *Single-Breasted Navy Blue Blazer*

Get it in summer weight so you can wear it year round, and buy a cheap one. Fit and material don't matter. Blazers are judged by their buttons only. Go to a Junior League charity bazaar in a wealthy neighborhood, and snip the fancy buttons off a used blazer—no purchase necessary. A blue blazer and dark-gray pants can be worn anywhere. At a formal dress ball just say, "I came straight from my boat and didn't have time to change."

### 3. White Chino Work Pants from Sears

Wear these with the blazer for convincing summer elegance. And you can admit you bought them at Sears. Rich people love a bargain. "How fabulous," they'll say. "Where is this Sear fellow's shop?"

### 4. Pair of Black Calf-Length Socks to be Washed Out Every Week or So

Rich men's pants don't fit well enough for them to wear interesting socks.

### 5. White Dress Shirt with French Cuffs

Also to be washed out every so often. Wear your blazer buttoned up at all times and you'll only have to iron a couple of inches down the shirtfront. Brass paper fasteners at 79¢ per hundred make handsome cuff links. With your blazer buttoned up and your French cuffs pulled down, you won't need any accessories like belts or wristwatches.

## 6. *Pair of Black Thom McAn Loafers*

Use kitchen matches to burn out the offending trademark. You can go too far with this bargain stuff.

## 7. *Pair of Cheap Rubber-Soled White Canvas Oxfords*

If you're going to be friends with the rich, you'll have to have something that won't mar their boat decks. And use these shoes for all sports, too. When you play tennis in long white pants and a white dress shirt with the sleeves rolled up, you will look like something out of *Chariots of Fire* and will be thought very fashionable.

## 8. *One Expensive Necktie*

With all the money you've just saved on clothes, you should be able to afford this. As mentioned in the accompanying text, it's the only piece of wearing apparel rich men notice anyway. And, if you're any good with rich women, your clothes will be in a pile on the floor before they get a good chance to look at them.

## FORMAL CLOTHES

The two most rented-looking things in the world are a rented woman and a rented tuxedo. The best you can do, if you don't own your own tuxedo, is to insist on the plainest and most conservative rental wear with a shawl collar and white shirt with simple pleats. Then rub mothballs all over it. All privately owned formal clothes stink of mothballs because rich men hate to get dressed up as much as other men do and usually haven't worn their tux since the last Lyme Disease Fund Charity Ball. And don't call it a "tux." Call it a "dinner suit."

It's absolutely unthinkable to wear any color but black. If you wear a white dinner jacket, all the other guests will ask you to bring them drinks. If you wear a blue tuxedo or a velvet one, you'll be pestered all night with requests for the band.

Wear a satin bow tie that you tie yourself. Don't let it bother you if you don't know how to tie it. Just wear it around untied with your collar open. This makes you look as if you've been up for three nights in a row having a hell of a time.

The correct shoes for formal wear are incredibly peculiar patent-leather dancing pumps with bows on them. All rich men have a pair of these, but they can never find them, so any black shoes will do.

## GROOMING

Looking rich takes more than clothes; you have to groom yourself like a rich man, too. But this is easy because rich

246

men aren't very well groomed. They don't care if they're dirty, as long as it doesn't look like hard-work dirt. So just make sure your fingernails are clean. And be sure to shave every day. Facial hair is for the insecure, who feel they have to hide acne, weak chins, and the like.

What kind of soap and cologne you use doesn't matter when you don't bathe very often, but you do have to have the right tan. A rich man's tan is not the kind you get from tanning salons or from simply lying in the sun. The rich have a harsh, peeling, year-round tan that comes from skiing, sailing, and drinking so much that all the blood vessels in their faces burst. The way to get one of these is to rub some sort of mild chemical irritant, like vinegar, on your face every morning and hang your head out the car window on your way to work.

Rich men's hair is more difficult to ape. Rich men are always exactly two months overdue for a haircut. No one knows how they accomplish this. All you can do by way of imitation is to get your hair cut four times a year and stay inside for a month every time you do.

## JEWELRY AND ACCESSORIES

There are only two things a rich man ever has hanging around his throat: military dog tags and a noose. Male jewelry is strictly for the bourgeoisie. Rich people know about money. They know what it's good for. Why would they buy gold ID bracelets when there's a takeover battle looming at RJR/ Nabisco and they could spend the money on skyrocketing stock shares instead?

Cuff links and wristwatches are the two acceptable types of

jewelry for rich men. An occasional gold signet ring is also seen, but unless you know—quick, off the top of your head— what your signet is, you'd better avoid that. Even wedding rings are considered a little déclassé. But don't take yours off if you've been wearing it for fifteen years. It'll leave a vivid white circle, and you'll look like you're out cheating on your wife for the evening. If you're rich enough, women don't care whether you're married.

Cuff links should be small and unobtrusive. Get the old-fashioned double-link kind. Never wear the type that have a little bar in the back. Those show that you don't have a valet to put your cuff links in for you.

Any plain, round, simple wristwatch on a leather or gros-grain band will do. Expandable metal watchbands look like you're about to shove your watch up your arm to keep it out of the way of the drill press or something. Never wear a digital wristwatch. Rich people neither know nor care *exactly* what time it is.

Other accessories should be kept to a minimum. A chrome Zippo is better than a fancy lighter, and better than a Zippo is a small box of wooden matches stolen from a good men's club.

Belts should not have buckles the size of hubcaps or your name across the back, especially not misspelled by your son at summer camp. Other personalizations, such as monograms and so on, should also be eschewed. If you're anyone important, people already know who you are. If you're not anyone important, there's no sense advertising it.

Handkerchiefs should be plain white cotton. Display one in your breast pocket at nightclubs and dinner dances. For more serious occasions, put your horn-rim glasses in your breast pocket, leaving one earpiece hanging outside your coat. This reminds others that you may have to read an important telex or vital deal memo at any moment—very smart looking.

Leave your wallet home. The world is open to rich people. They don't have to carry a lot of cash and fancy credit cards. Besides, the rich love money too well to be spendthrifts. They delight in getting others to pick up the tab, which is why it's not only polite, but also very delightful to imitate them.

# 27

# Women's Clothes

*Taste is the feminine of genius.*
> —Edward FitzGerald

The subject of women's clothes is beyond the scope of a guide to etiquette or any other kind of book. There are mysteries to female costume and body decoration that will never be plumbed by the human mind. Why, for instance, do women paint their lips, eyes, and the tips of their fingers and toes but not their noses, ears, or elbows? Also, just what is the connection between women's shoe styles and U.S. foreign policy? No one has ever figured out the reason, but a fashion for high heels and open-toed footwear means a strong anticommunist stance in Europe, while boots and sandals mean an even stronger anticommunist stance in Asia. Wedge heels and platform soles indicate concern for human rights combined with confusion over foreign-policy goals, and sensible shoes show all-out war is on the way.

What all this has to do with manners is anyone's guess. But common courtesy dictates that we accept the situation as it is because there's no cure for women and clothes.

## RULES FOR WOMEN'S CLOTHES

One might as well tell the tide when to rise or order quarks and leptons around inside an atom as lay down rules of decorum for female dress. Nonetheless, a few general guidelines can be posited for the aid of orphan girls being raised by male relatives, former men recuperating from sex change operations, novice transvestites, and others not fully practiced at being women.

- A woman should dress to excite. Dressing very slowly when you're late to a movie, for instance, excites husbands to a fury.
- A woman should dress to attract attention. To attract the most attention, a woman should be either nude or wearing something as expensive as getting her nude is going to be.
- Always adhere to the rules of proportion when dressing:
  1. No jewelry bigger than your dog
  2. No dog smaller than your purse
  3. No purse larger in diagonal measurement than your waist is in circumference

4. No pants on waists larger than diagonal measurement of purse + dog + earrings

- Do not expose so much of a good body that it gives your father a heart attack.
- Do not expose so much of a bad body that it gives your husband ideas about leaving home.
- Your jewelry should not drag on the ground behind you.
- Remember that the purpose of women's underwear is to cover all parts of the body except the breasts, buttocks, and genital area. Sort of.
- If your hair is less than one eighth of an inch long, make sure you have a skull tan.

(All these rules may be disregarded if Paris *Vogue* says it's okay or if you feel like it or for any other reason.)

## RULES FOR MEN WHEN WOMEN ARE WEARING CLOTHES AROUND THEM

- Never tell a woman she looks good in something. She'll want to know what was wrong with what she was wearing before.
- Never tell a woman she looks bad in something. She'll cry.
- Never tell a woman another woman looks good in something. She'll be jealous.
- Never tell a woman another woman looks bad in something. She probably owns one just like it.
- Never forget, women's favorite topic of conversation is clothes. Be sure to talk about clothes a lot with women.

## GETTING THE RIGHT LOOK FOR THE RIGHT OCCASION

Use the following hints to properly coordinate your appearance with your day-to-day activities.

### *Look Good . . .*

Whenever you've just done something bad like taking your ex-husband for everything he was worth in divorce court. (Looking good will get you more husbands.)

### *Look Bad . . .*

Whenever you've just done something good like raise ten children or cook dinner for fifty. (Looking bad will get you sympathy.)

### *Look Sexy . . .*

At work or any other time when it's impossible to have sex. (This gets men excited.)

### *Look Unsexy . . .*

Right before bed. (This gets your hair ready so you can look sexy at work again tomorrow.)

# CLOTHES PURCHASING TIPS FOR WOMEN

## *How to Get a Proper Fit*

Buy clothes in whatever size you think is cute and then throw up after every meal until they fit you.

## *How to Get a Proper Fit in Jeans*

This is not a problem. Jeans only come in one size, which is why they're always baggy on slim, attractive girls and skintight on great big fat ones.

# DETERMINING HOW MANY PIERCED EARRINGS TO WEAR

In order to determine how many pierced earrings to wear, start with the number two and add one earring for each of the following phrases that accurately describes your life:
• Bulimia
• Drug dependency
• Sexual promiscuity
• From Queens
• Boyfriend in a band
Now subtract one earring for each of the following phrases that you answer yes to:
• I just took my LSATs.
• My parents are on their way for a visit.
• I have a church wedding coming up.

# 28

# Clothes for Adolescents, Mental Patients, and Members of Rock and Roll Bands

Brown shoes don't make it.

—Frank Zappa

The wearing of weird clothes by young people is a tradition dating back to the days of Shelley, Keats, and Byron. They used to dress up in Greek bedsheets and go around yelling, "Hail to thee, blithe spirit! Bird thou never wert"—pretty tame by today's standards, but considered alarming in 1821.

As with many enduring traditions, weird clothes on teens serve a number of social functions. Weird young-people apparel is helpful to adults, making teen-agers easier to spot and avoid. Thus we may escape the frequent stupid fads and constant emotional problems of the young.

Weird clothes are also helpful to teens themselves, making it easier for them to fend off sexual advances from older people. A certain type of older person, with more aesthetics than sense, is drawn to the beauty and vitality of teen-agers. But, on closer inspection, the older person will see that the teen-agers are covered in vegetable dye, feathers, denim things, and that it isn't easy to tell if they are girls or what, and he will leave them alone.

Another function of strange youthful clothing is to help fight racism. When ordinary white middle-class kids dress in an astonishing and highly irritating manner, it gives the police and uneducated southerners someone new to pick on. This takes the heat off Negroes, Hispanics, and Jews.

But the most important thing that adolescent dress peculiarities accomplish is that they shock parents. On the face of it, this would seem to be a rude thing to do. But, actually, it's very courteous and nice. When a boy comes home from school wearing blue hair, pedal pushers, and a pair of bowling shoes, of course his parents are shocked. But this is a mild kind of shock, and not only will the parents recover from it, but it will help prepare them mentally and physically for the much worse shocks the child is going to give them in later life—when he is indicted for running a child prostitution ring or is written up in *Newsweek* as the person who gave the fatal dose of crack to David and Julie Eisenhower. If it were not for the preliminary sartorial shocks delivered in earlier years, the parents might suffer coronaries or some other kind of breakdown.

# A TEEN-AGE CLOTHING DILEMMA

Weird clothing is *de rigueur* for teen-agers, but today's generation of teens is finding is difficult to be sufficiently weird. This is because the previous generations of teens, who went through adolescence in the 60s and 70s, used up practically all the available weirdness. After what went on in that twenty-five-year period, almost nothing looks strange to anyone. A contemporary teen-ager's mother will return from a Plasmatics concert featuring Wendy O. Williams and ask her daughter, "What about flesh-colored latex Capri pants and nipple Band-Aids—would it look good on me?"

Of course, this is only one aspect of a broader problem in our society. Teens are finding it increasingly hard to upset the editorial-page writers at *The New York Times* and to get sensational photo spreads done about them in *Life* magazine. And they are not taking nearly as many drugs as kids used to. This is not because they don't want to take drugs but there are some drugs kids don't take today because their parents took them all and there aren't any left.

## A POSSIBLE SOLUTION

A possible solution to the problem of "used-weird" facing modern young people would be for everyone between the ages of seventeen and twenty to join the United States Army. The U.S. Army has very weird clothes. Also, this would shock everyone's parents. *The New York Times* editorial-page writers would be deeply perplexed and *Life* would be sure to do a sensational photo spread. Besides, there is supposed to be a terrific availability of drugs in the military.

# Section VII

## THE LEISURE EFFORT

*Why, do nothing, be like a gentleman, be idle. . . .*
—George Chapman

# 29

## Sports Manners

*For what do we live, but to make sport for our
neighbors, and laugh at them in our turn?*

—Jane Austen

*M*any people who are nor-
mally polite turn discourteous and rude on the playing field.
Etiquette should have a guiding role in all aspects of life. Good
manners shouldn't be reserved only for social occasions such
as making a living. Good manners should also have a place in
the serious business of life, which is fooling around.

The most important part of sports is winning. Therefore
it's imperative for a courteous sportsman to be a good winner.
A good winner always praises the efforts of his opponent. He
says something like "I'm sure you would have beaten me,

Frank, if you weren't so fat." And a good winner is an honest winner. He says, "You notice that I still beat you, Frank, even though you lied about the ball being out of bounds." And a good winner never takes advantage of a lesser opponent: "Let's make it double or nothing this time, Frank—that way you'll have a chance to get your money back."

Naturally it's also important to be a good loser. A good loser swears loudly, throws his sports equipment on the ground, and kicks any small animals or children nearby. If a loser doesn't do these things he deprives the winner of most of winning's pleasure.

## THE POPULAR NEW "LITE" SPORTS

Winning is such an important part of sports that it's often considered rude not to. As a result, a number of modern sports have been developed in which everyone wins—or, at least, no one doesn't. These are called "lite" sports because they contain smaller amounts of potential embarrassment. Such sports are particularly popular with the middle classes, who are not used to large amounts of leisure time and are just learning how to goof off.

## Video Games

The most popular of the new sports is video-game playing. Video games represent something of a courtesy landmark because they make it socially acceptable, in a sporting context, to eat Twinkies, never go outdoors, have a terrible complexion, and be able to operate a computer. Video games are also delightful because there is something about a television that fights back which is so perfectly appropriate to our society.

## *Running*

After video games, the second most popular new sport is running. This is not running in the traditional track-and-field sense or running because someone is chasing you, but an entirely new sport which consists of running from nothing to nowhere. It's truly impossible to lose at this. But an even more genteel thing about running is the polite conversation that results. Nothing is more suitable to the well-mannered modern intellect than a discussion among a group of runners:

"Well, I ran today."

"Me, too."

"I ran yesterday—three miles."

"I ran four miles today."

"I ran four miles yesterday but tomorrow I'm going to run five."

"I think I'll run four miles again tomorrow, but I might run five miles myself."

And so on.

Like the conversation it inspires, the rules of running are simple:

1. Don't run in street clothes or while carrying bags or packages—it makes you look as though you just robbed a store.

2. Women with breasts larger than their heads should use a Nautilus machine instead.

3. If you run more than twenty miles a week, try not to die young. It will make people snigger.

## *Frisbee Playing*

A third new sport, Frisbee playing, is not only impossible to lose at but is also remarkably polite because it's so hard to break things with a Frisbee. Just say "excuse me" to everyone you hit. The Frisbee is closely related to the Wiffle ball in its noncompetitive, nondestructive qualities and may be seen as a step toward fulfilling the ultimate promise of the modern world—the creation of a "Wiffle life" in which nothing serious ever happens.

Frisbee playing is also more intellectual than are traditional sports. All the "lite sports" have a tendency to introduce an intellectual element into athletics. This shows great consideration for the clumsy pizza-faced smart people the world is full of. Playing Frisbee with a Frisbee-catching dog allows for an especially large display of intelligence. It shows that the Frisbee player is too smart to play something like football or ice hockey, in which he might get injured, and it shows that the dog is too smart to throw the Frisbee back.

# GOLF

New sports have won many adherents, but traditional sports continue to be popular because it's hard to get Frisbee players to make bets and their dogs don't usually carry cash. The other new sports are also difficult to gamble on. It seems cruel to make a wager about who'll look most like death warmed over after running for twenty minutes. And, as for video games, no grown man likes to lose a shoebox full of quarters to a ten-year-old.

Many traditional sports have other virtues besides betting opportunities. Golf, for instance, combines two favorite American pastimes: taking long walks and hitting things with a stick. Try to tailor your golfing behavior to the low-key, low-pressure spirit of these antecedents. Calm the nerves of fellow players by talking cheerfully to them while they tee off or attempt to one-putt. Help the greenskeeper do his job by making sure that grass roots are well aerated with divots. Give the caddy a chance to catch up on his aerobic exercises trotting alongside the golf cart with your bag on his shoulder. And don't hit things you aren't supposed to. An important aspect of golf is knowing what to hit.

## Things You Are Allowed to Hit in Golf

- Golf balls
- Golf balls with your shoe accidentally because the golf ball's lie was so bad you couldn't see it and kicked it out onto the fairway by accident
- Trees, fence posts, and marker flags after you miss a shot

- The bottle
- Yourself in the head

## *Things You Are Not Allowed to Hit in Golf*

- People in the foursome ahead of you, if one of them is likely to blackball any of your business clients at the club
- Your boss
- The caddy, if he's anybody's son

## SKIING

The sport of skiing consists of wearing three thousand dollars' worth of clothes and equipment and driving two hundred miles in the snow in order to stand around at a bar and get drunk.

Some people go out on the slopes, too, but this is not considered in the best of taste because slush gets tracked into the lodge. The best skiing is always done on "mahogany ridge."

If you do go out on the slopes, remember that long lift lines are skiing's most common annoyance. Cut right in at the front of them and get yourself on the chair lift immediately so that you aren't part of the lift-line problem.

# TENNIS

Tennis has been discovered by people who are supposed to be bowling. The world is severely in need of relief from tennis. Do what you can by organizing games to be played on horseback. This will ruin almost any all-weather court and eliminate further tennis playing. Or you can insist on playing some more polite variation, like armchair tennis. Armchair tennis is played by two opponents seated on either side of the court in comfortable armchairs. Each player has a huge pitcher of drinks and a hundred cans of tennis balls. Neither is permitted to rise from his seat to return a shot. The player who has to go to the bathroom first loses.

# OTHER RACKET SPORTS

Squash, racquetball, paddleball, and other indoor modifications of tennis are to tennis itself what secret homosexuality is to the gay rights movement—an improvement, but no remedy. An end can be put to most of these games by firing a golf ball into the court enclosures with a powerful slingshot.

As for handball—the idea of playing racket sports without even a racket is too ludicrous for discussion.

# SOFTBALL

There is nothing to say about softball as a sport. No one has ever paid enough attention either while watching or playing to be able to remember anything about it.

The interesting aspect of softball is putting together the teams and matching them up for games. In American society, any time a group gets its own softball team, the members of that group feel legitimate and recognized and begin to function as a normal part of the social fabric. Black, Chicano, gay, and homeless softball teams have formed in various cities and play teams from the police and fire departments. The result is better minority relations. The Weather Underground is now a softball team with games scheduled against the FBI and several grand juries. And there are plans afoot to turn the U.S. Congress into a team and let them play decent people in hopes they'll begin to behave, too.

## VOLLEYBALL

The purpose of volleyball is to get your sexual parts to flop around. It isn't really much good unless played in the nude. The rule, cited for running, about women with breasts bigger than their heads, may be suspended for volleyball. Women with huge breasts should not run because running women make terrible faces and the combination of scary facial expression and immense jiggling breasts is liable to cause sexual confusion in preadolescent boys. Volleyball players, however, usually look like they're having a wonderful time and so may jiggle as much as they want without adverse psychological effects on members of the audience. In fact, if you're going to play volleyball, you'd better make sure your sexual parts are large enough to flop around in an impressive way. An exception might be made for large, floppy asses. People with large, floppy asses really shouldn't participate in any sports. They especially shouldn't ride bicycles, because it makes people laugh so hard that they lose control of their automobiles.

## HORSEBACK RIDING

The term "horseback riding" covers a wide variety of athletic activities. All types of horseback riding, however, should be done on a horse. Doing them on a naked girl in a motel room is a different sport entirely, even if she lets you use spurs.

Mounting is the first step to horseback riding. The rule about mounting a horse is to do so. You will look very foolish prancing around a show ring or clearing a fence in hunting pinks if you don't have a horse under you. It is also important to mount the middle top part of a horse. If you mount the horse anywhere else you're bound to get in its way and it in yours.

Every type of horseback riding has its own customs and manners. Space does not allow for detailing all the specifics. Riding etiquette tends to be complex and difficult to learn. For example, consider the matter of the stirrup cup at a fox hunt. Just try drinking out of a stirrup.

Briefly, however, there are two principal types of riding in the United States: English and western. In English riding you don't have anything to hold on to and in western riding you do but they make fun of you if you use it. Don't wear chaps or carry a Winchester .30-30 when you ride English style, and don't wear a top hat and blow a French horn when riding western style. Don't wear a motorcycle helmet when you do either. It's a perfectly good idea, but it just isn't done.

## HUNTING AND FISHING

Hunting and fishing are the ways polite society gets the urge to murder out of its system. If your bloodlust is not being fully satisfied by these sports, maybe you should go a step further and pluck birds or gut deer *before* you kill them.

A polite hunter, however, is not deaf to the pleas of animal lovers. Unless you are completely overcome by the desire to kill and maim, you should do everything you can to make hunting more comfortable for the animals. Shoot ducks on the water and pheasants on the ground so they will not have a long, painful fall after they are hit. Use shelled corn and salt licks to allow deer a last meal before their demise. And shoot them right there where the bait is so that they won't have to walk a long way while full. And be sure to drink before hunting to give the animals a sporting chance to see some humans killed.

But when you're fishing, these niceties of behavior may be abandoned. Fish are not smart enough to care about courtesy or sportsmanship, not even trout. Go ahead and kill them with hand grenades if you get tired of screwing around with dry flies.

# GAMBLING

Hunting is a replacement for murder. Gambling is a replacement for entrepreneurial vigor and inventiveness. Entrepreneurial vigor and inventiveness are old-fashioned and don't leave time enough for the social graces. Thomas Edison and Henry Ford hardly ever got the chance to kick back on the waterbed, scarf some Chinese takeout, and listen to the new U2 album. They would have been a lot cooler heads if they'd made their money playing blackjack.

Gambling is the hallmark of a truly polite society. Just ask Prince Rainier. Prince Rainier will also tell you that gambling debts are debts of honor and should be paid before any others, especially before debts owed to companies that used to be owned by Thomas Edison and Henry Ford. Car salesmen and electric-company meter readers rarely break your legs for being rude.

# WEIGHT-LIFTING, BODY BUILDING, AND EXERCISE PROGRAMS

Exercise programs are the blue-collar equivalents of gambling. Instead of capitalism, they take the place of hard work. Hard work, of course, is always out of fashion.

# MARATHON RUNNING, LONG-DISTANCE SWIMMING, BICYCLE RACING, AND OTHER ENDURANCE SPORTS

The abolition of hard work and entrepreneurial vigor has left voids in our society, and so has the abolition of pain. Endurance sports provide people with the pain they seem to be missing from modern dentistry and health care. Of course it's also natural that in a self-actuated, self-aware society like our own we would want some kind of pain that was self-inflicted. It's like the death penalty, which is most vigorously protested by the same kind of person who usually commits suicide.

Anyway, endurance sports provide polite, fashionable pain, which is especially satisfying to sensible people because the participants in endurance sports are so stupid. Marathon runners say they run because "it makes me feel better about myself." More intelligent people do things that make *others* feel better about *them*. What's the difference how you feel about yourself? You're probably not in a position to give yourself a raise.

# DANGEROUS SPORTS

The only polite thing to do when engaged in sky diving, hang gliding, ice climbing, or any other dangerous sport is die. That's what everyone's waiting around for.

## GAMES

Games, such as checkers, chess, darts, and backgammon, should always be played for money. Otherwise the stakes are psychological. You're betting you can humiliate someone and make him look like a fool. This is disgusting. No gentle person stoops to behavior like this unless he can make a buck at it.

## TRULY ENJOYABLE SPORTS

Some sports, such as croquet, pool, badminton, and touch football, are actually a lot of fun to play. Unfortunately, playing sports for fun is quite out of fashion at the moment. Perhaps this is because modern people are doing so many other things—divorcing, developing drug habits, screwing up their children—for fun. In order to make fun sports socially acceptable, they must be played in deadly earnest and practiced in secret and argued over loudly.

## SILLY SPORTS

Bowling, basketball, stickball, putt-putt golf, and so on are silly sports. They should be avoided by modern people, who are plenty silly enough already. Be particularly careful to avoid basketball if you are white, under five foot nine, and over twenty-five—nothing's as silly as that.

Some silly sports, such as bowling and putt-putt golf, can

still be played if you're careful to make it clear that you've never played them before and don't have the slightest idea how they're done. Bring your drivers to the putt-putt course and tee off for all you're worth. Or put the bowling ball under your arm and run down the alley and kick it over the pins. You won't look any less silly this way but at least you'll get it established that you don't belong to the social class which takes these sports seriously.

# 30

## Travel Etiquette

*The wogs begin at Calais.*

—English Saying

There's no reason to behave any differently from normal when you travel. In fact, there's no reason to behave at all. You're never going to see these people again, so what do you care? But, if you feel like being nice, be nice in the normal way. Foreigners are just the same as regular people if you count bucketheads, gooks, and wops as regular.

Foreigners will always be nice to you. Everybody admires Americans, as well they should. Give them more reasons to admire Americans. Show what a happy, powerful, and hearty people we are by taking up lots of space and making plenty of noise when you're abroad.

## LANGUAGE

Etiquette is a universal language. And so is English. Foreigners may pretend otherwise, but if English is spoken loudly enough, anyone can understand it, the British included. Actually, there's no such thing as a foreign language. The world is just filled with people who grunt and squeak instead of speaking sensibly. French may be an exception. But since it's impossible to figure out what French people are saying, we'll never know for sure.

True, some grunts and squeaks carry a sort of meaning to the people who utter them. It can be amusing to learn the sounds some foreigners make when they're trying to say "hello":

French: *"Bonjour"*

Italian: *"Buon giorno"*

Spanish: *"Tu madre es una puta"*

But learning more is unnecessary. It only encourages them in their ignorant ways. Real communication should be conducted in English or by waving around fistfuls of the packing tissue and candy wrappers foreign people use for currency.

# GENERAL DIFFERENCES BETWEEN FOREIGN AND AMERICAN ETIQUETTE

Although most courtesies are the same the world over, there are a few general differences between foreign and American manners. For one thing, foreigners always consider it good form to haggle over prices, even at airline ticket counters. For another thing, tips are usually added to your bill, so you never have to tip anyone when you're traveling overseas. It is fun, however, to carry around the smallest denomination of foreign coins and tip natives with one of them just to hear the full range of noises that foreigners can make. But by no means should you follow the American practice of tipping people according to what their services are worth. You'd have to carry around a big sack full of spoiled fish or old unmatched socks to accomplish this in most foreign countries.

Whether you adopt foreign manners or not, getting along in other countries is always easier if you have a sense of humor. Most foreigners have a great sense of humor themselves and enjoy being part of the fun when you laugh at the way they dress and act.

# SPECIFIC DIFFERENCES BETWEEN FOREIGN AND AMERICAN ETIQUETTE

Many countries have etiquette peculiarities of their own. You may want to conform to the foreign idea of good behavior. Foreigners have feelings, too, even if they do lack any means of articulating them.

# England

The English have only recently become foreigners and aren't very good at it yet. This is why they make such lousy gigolos. This is also why they expect to be regarded as equals. Therefore, treat them as you would any American with a severe speech defect.

# Spain

The Spanish enjoy teasing domestic animals, not only bulls but other barnyard creatures as well. They think it's quite merry if you kick their dogs, throw stones at their burros, and chase their chickens around with a stick.

# Italy

When having an audience with the Pope, devout Catholics kiss his foot. If you are a *very* devout Catholic you may want to kiss some other part of him. Go ahead and try, he won't think you're queer. Then again, the Pope is not an Italian. An Italian *will* think you're queer if you don't make a pass at his wife. And everyone in the country will be deeply offended if you don't pinch a lot of women while you're there.

# Germany

Because of their cuisine, Germans don't consider farting rude. They'd certainly be out of luck if they did.

# France

The French consider it good manners to burp after meals and wipe your behind with your hand. Or maybe that's the Arabs. You'll have to experiment and see. Anyway, while you're in France, touch all the paintings in the Louvre to make sure they're real. The French will want to know if they aren't.

# Israel

Israelis love practical jokes such as switching countries on the Palestinians and so on. When you go to Israel, tape some railroad flares to an old alarm clock and hide this in your luggage.

# China

Anyplace where dogs are food, you're probably supposed to treat your food like a house pet. When given a bowl of rice, stroke it, talk to it, and take it outside for a walk before you eat.

# Turkey

Don't bend over in Turkey. Who knows what they might think it's a polite invitation to do?

# Japan

The Japanese are very small and it bothers them. So you should act as small as you can yourself. Wear clothes that are three or four sizes too big and ask Japanese to lift you up so you can reach drinking fountains.

*Etiquette is for people who have no breeding;
fashion is for those who have no taste.*
—Colonel Chiswell Langhorne